D0803356

A Priest Forever

A PRIEST FOREVER

Carter Heyward

HARPER & ROW, PUBLISHERS

New York, Hagerstown, San Francisco, London

ILLUSTRATION CREDITS

PHOTOGRAPHS

Bruce Rodgers: page 19; Jackie Gill: 36; David Doely: 44; New York Times: 60; Brad Hess: jacket and page 87; Paul W. Mikels: 127.

CARTOON

Rog Bollen, "Animals Crackers." Reprinted by permission of the Chicago Tribune-New York News Syndicate, Inc. Copyright 1974. All rights reserved. page 16.

Library of Congress Cataloging in Publication Data

Heyward, Carter.
  A priest forever.
  Includes bibliographical references.
  1. Heyward, Carter. 2. Ordination of women—
Protestant Episcopal Church in the U.S.A. I. Title.
BX5995.H46A34 1976   283'.092'4   [B]   75–36736
ISBN 0–06–063893–1

76 77 78 79 80 10 9 8 7 6 5 4 3 2 1

ACKNOWLEDGEMENTS

Many people have been helpful in the publication of this book.

My Union Theological Seminary colleagues who stood steadily with me in the aftermath of the Philadelphia ordinations were significant to the book's development—especially my students in "Feminism and Vocation" and "Women in Ministry"; as well as Jean Gilbert, Susan Savell, Georgia Wilcoxson, Norma Barsness, Jim Bergland, Sally Bentley, Tom F. Driver, Linda Clark, Beverly Harrison, Sidney Skirvin, Lee Hancock, Jean Lambert, Connie Baugh, Barbara Wheeler, and Tony Ruger.

I think also of Thelma Pyle, who answered the phone so that I could write; of Bob Svenson, Arthur Tingue, and Virginia Wink, who have helped me begin to claim the honesty, humor, and courage to live (and tell) my own story, and of Robert DeWitt, who has shown me what authority is.

My sister priests—especially Alison Cheek, my "partner in the 'ecclesiastical crime' of celebration," and Sue Hiatt, my apartment-mate—have offered empathy and encouragement throughout the preparation of this manuscript, my brother priest, Peter Beebe, too.

During the past few years others too have contributed to this process in ways that they may not realize—among them Caci Cole, David Conolly, Ann Elliot, Bart Sherman, John Craig, Susan Thornton, Leslie Pederson, Nancy Scheibner, my sister Ann, my brother Robbie, my father Bob, and my mother Mary Ann.

Finally, my appreciation to my editor, Marie Cantlon; to Brad Hess, photographer; to Liz Jones, who typed the final copy; to my uncle Luther Carter, Barbara Elden, Jill Thompson, Emily Hewitt, Betty Mosley, Pattie Handloss, Kay Longcope for their editorial assistance; and to Eileen Jones, whose vision has helped me shape the soul of the book.

Carter Heyward
Cambridge, Massachusetts
August, 1975

For my sister priests

Holy God, we have left undone those things
which we ought to have done, and we have done
those things which we ought not to have done.

Yet, by thy grace, there is health in us!

In thy mystery, carry us on.
As we bring unity and joy, humble us.
As we bring division and pain, forgive us.
  In our struggling, strengthen us.
  In our stumbling, lift us.
    When we weep, comfort us.
    When we laugh, enjoy us.

             Amen.

Now if perfection had been attainable through the Levitical priesthood (for under it the people received the law), what further need would there have been for another priest to arise after the order of Melchizedek,* rather than one named after the order of Aaron? For when there is a change in the priesthood, there is necessarily a change in the law as well. For the one of whom these things are spoken belonged to another tribe, from which no one has ever served at the altar. For it is evident that our Lord was descended from Judah, and in connection with that tribe Moses said nothing about priests.

This becomes even more evident when another priest arises in the likeness of Melchizedek, who has become a priest, not according to a legal requirement concerning bodily descent but by the power of an indestructible life. For it is witnessed of him,

"Thou art a priest for ever, after the order of Melchizedek."

On the one hand, a former commandment is set aside because of its weakness and uselessness (for the law made nothing perfect); on the other hand, a better hope is introduced, through which we draw near to God.

Hebrews 7:11–19**

---

* See Genesis 14:18, Psalm 110:4, and Hebrews 5:5–10; 6:13–7:28. "For this Melchizedek, king of Salem, priest of the most high God, met Abraham returning from the slaughter of the kings and blessed him; and to him Abraham apportioned a tenth part of everything. He is first, by translation of his name, king of righteousness, and then he is also king of Salem, that is, king of peace. He is without father or mother, or genealogy, and has neither beginning of days nor end of life, but resembling the Son of God he continues a priest forever" (Hebrews 7:1–3).

** Unless otherwise indicated, quotations from Scripture are from Revised Standard Version *Bible*.

A Priest Forever

And Jesus said to them, "Follow me."
Mark 1:17a

FOR THE SAKE OF THE UNITY OF THE CHURCH AND THE CAUSE OF
ORDINATION OF WOMEN TO THE PRIESTHOOD I BEG YOU TO RECONSIDER
YOUR INTENTION TO PRESENT YOURSELF FOR ORDINATION BEFORE THE
NECESSARY CANONICAL CHANGES ARE MADE. AM DEEPLY CONCERNED
ABOUT THE RELATIONSHIP OBSTACLES WHICH CAN RESULT WITHIN YOUR
DIOCESE AS WELL AS IN THE CHURCH AS A WHOLE.
—Telegram from John M. Allin, Presiding Bishop
of the Episcopal Church, to eleven women
deacons, July 23, 1974.

Dear Bishop Allin:

I have received your telegram. Each day I am reconsidering my
intention to be ordained, God willing, on July 29. This is a time of
prayer. If I do proceed with plans as scheduled, as I intend to at
this point, it will be for the sake of the unity of humankind in
Christ. My hope is that the Episcopal Church, of which I am fond
and to which I have committed myself professionally, will follow
suit on this particular "issue" of women's ordination. You have my
prayers. I ask for yours.

Sincerely,
Carter Heyward
July 25, 1974

And so it was that on July 29, 1974, the Feast Day of Mary
and Martha of Bethany, something happened in the Episcopal
Church that set shock waves in motion throughout the Christian
Church. Church people came together and acted on convictions
that had been born and nurtured within the Church itself. Somewhere within our corporate religious past, we had been taught

that all women and men are people of God; that any person of God can be called to any ministry in the Church; moreover, that God compels us to act again and again for whatever is just and decent.

The Church had told us something it apparently had not meant us to hear. But in Philadelphia's Church of the Advocate, hundreds of Episcopalians, joined in Spirit by people throughout the world, came together to celebrate the Good News we had heard. Called by God to the vocation of priesthood, affirmed in this call by Episcopal parishes and, *de facto*, by dioceses (large clusters of parishes), eleven Episcopal women deacons were ordained priests by two retired and one resigned Episcopal bishops in the presence of over 1,500 people.

Praised and criticized; admired and despised; accepted by some, ignored and rejected by others, the "Philadelphia Eleven" may well never have come together had not a common God compelled us toward a common vocation and a common moment. We are women with different personalities, backgrounds, experiences, ministries, and perspectives. We respect and value our diversity. Although much of what I write could have been penned by my sister priests, I cannot speak for them.

In writing "theology"—i.e. about one's relationship to God— the theologian must in all fairness to her readers, give some idea of her purpose: To whom is she writing, and why?

I write to any woman, man, boy, or girl, who is interested in the current Episcopal controversy over women priests. I write also to any person who is exploring his or her own relationship to God, whatever the person conceives "God" to be. I write especially to *women* who have something of themselves invested in religious institutions, particularly the Christian Church.

My purpose in writing is to tell my story, in the hope of stimulating the readers to tell their own. Central to my story is a theme: That I, a woman, not only have had since birth a right to be eligible for ordination to the priesthood; but moreover along with all women and men, a right to choose and shape my own life; a responsibility in fact to claim my own authority and live accordingly. No one can deny me this right, or bear the burden of this responsibility for me.

It is easy to be persuaded that, if a woman demands radical autonomy and self-determination, there can be no place for her in such institutions as the Church. If this were true, I would have to maintain that any institution which must thrive on my unfulfilled being—my submissiveness, my nonassertiveness—is an institution that has outlived its value in my life. But I am not persuaded that this is true.

I see women as the single most creative force within the Christian Church. We, as a group, are those challenged most immediately with the task of *renewal*—of making new what is old—within and beyond ourselves in the Church and elsewhere.

We are asked to bring something new to the world around us—as workers, wives, daughters, mothers, scholars, artists, politicians, priests. *We are called to tell our stories*, and in telling our stories *we manifest a new reality*—the new reality of being female *and* speaking up *and* being heard *and* reshaping—on the basis of who we are—those institutions that matter most to us. Where we cannot be heard and where we cannot reshape, we are called to the reality of building new community.

The woman with a story to tell in the Christian Church is the new theologian. We pick up where our sisters Mary Magdalene, Joanna, Mary the mother of James, and other women who witnessed to the Resurrection left off. With them, we tell of our theological experience, our relationship to God. With them, we insist that what we have to say is worth hearing. For we have been filled with the power of the Holy Spirit, and we are compelled to manifest, in whatever ways we can, the reality of God's presence.

> *Whether the church accepts you or not, you have in a very real sense already won the battle.*
> —Letter to me from seminary dean, summer, 1974.

My faith is in God:[1] mysterious process, creating new life, destroying old life within, between, and among us. A God of that which we see as "darkness" and "light." A God of that which we feel as "pain" and "joy." A God of that which we name as "good" and "bad." A God of that which we experience as "birth" and "death." A God in whose holy movement all contradictions are woven together into a unity and a peace not to be attained by human will, human knowledge, or human effort.

I see and know this God through the person of Jesus of Nazareth, a particular young Jewish male in whose being opposites coincided: humility and power; fear and courage; work and faith; suffering and peace; pain and joy; death and life; particularity and universality; humanity and divinity. Jesus of Nazareth, Jesus the Christ, who transcendent of time and space is here with us today, as we are with each other today, brothers and sisters here today, reaching for one another through pages of a book. Sharing our humanness and our relationship to that common God. Tedious Growth. Terrible Good, which passes all understanding.

I believe that this God here today and way beyond today is a Holy Spirit, weaving us together with threads of commonality. A Spirit in whose movement there is no barrier—neither color, nor ethnicity, nor class, nor nationality, nor sexuality, nor gender, nor ideology, nor religion, nor age. A Spirit whose community is humankind. Whose movement is irrepressible. Whose nature is not to be understood or categorized into doctrinal boxes.

I believe that we are created alone; and that we journey together alone, as simply human beings in community with human beings; and that all of us are called to rebirth and to re-formation even moment by moment. I believe that we were created to laugh, to weep, to dance, to stumble, to sing, to hide, to risk, to pray, to grieve, to leap in faith, to act decisively, to step back and rest, and to rejoice along the way. Thanks be to God in Christ, Christ in us, and us in God. Amen.

My experience on this small planet—my involvements and observations, relationships and estrangements, educational processes and work, other events in my life, and faith itself—has led me to marvel at how it is that so many layers of a single reality are interwoven, even when we can see only so little.

For me, life is sacrament: an outward and visible sign of an inward and spiritual grace. And *agapé* (a "love meal") is Holy Communion. Sacrament is very real to me, most all of the time; and wherever it is, it is substantial and it is valid. I agree with Jesuit theologian Juan Luis Segundo[2] who suggests that a "sacramental crisis" is threatening the Church. He continues: The crisis is *not* that we do not take such rites as baptism, communion, and ordination seriously enough. The crisis is that we do not take such concrete events as grocery shopping, studying, shooting pictures, making love, walking the dog, protesting injustice, and feeding the hungry *sacramentally enough*.

We are baptized to go forth into the world, rejoicing in the power of the Spirit, believing full well that at any moment (*kairos*), theology will be shaped to reflect, however inadequately, the movement of the Spirit among the human beings who are rejoicing in its power. Such theology—reflecting in a glass darkly what is actually happening among faithful human beings—is the conservation of future Church.

So my experience is teaching me.

Christian tradition is, for me, more problematic than my faith or my experience. It is more problematic for me *because* of my faith and my experience. For some people, tradition is a crutch; for me, it is a stumbling block, not yet so big that I can't get over it.

The temptation is always to throw out the baby with the bath —which is to say, in this case, to throw out the tradition taken as a whole rather than those parts of the tradition which are used so brutally and offensively against human beings.

And yet, I am in some important ways a traditionalist. History, continuity, and sacramental connections between all points of time and space, are very real to me. I find much joy in remembering our ancestors—like Sarah and Abraham. I'm grateful to them for what they have given us: our roots.

Perhaps because I find deep meaning in the tradition of our Judaeo-Christian, and Episcopal, community, I am especially sensitive to the hiddenness, the rejection, and the defilement various peoples have met within the tradition. In Christian tradition, this invisibility or violation has been to some great degree true for nonwhite people; for Jewish people; for non-Western people; for poor people; for homosexual people; and for female people.

As a *female*, I do not find much theology within the tradition that helps me make sense out of my experience as a woman along a continuum of past, present, and future women. For traditionally, the context of theology has been *male* experience. As a *female* attempting to discover her roots in the tradition, I look back and only occasionally see myself there: WOMAN— temptress, virginal mother, "gateway to the devil," "misbegotten seed," witch, saint: Everything but simply human.

To this I must say no. Because I am simply human.

With my sisters-in-Christ, I have had to go back again and look again and feel and think and explore again, to find out whether or not in fact our humanness *is* fully affirmed in Christ Jesus. If it is *not*, then not only are our *ordinations* to the priesthood "invalid," as the bishops have maintained, but also our *baptisms*; and Christianity becomes for us no more than a male construct, club, and caste. But if women's humanness *is* affirmed in Christ Jesus—despite predilections of Church Fathers on this matter—then not only our baptisms, but also our ordinations are valid. Real. Alive.

> *Of course you are a priest—unless there have never been any, can never be any, and the whole category is meaningless.*
> —Letter to me from woman religious (nun),
> Diocese of New York, summer, 1974.

Sophie Couch always wanted to be a priest. Perched in the apple tree, mischievously munching on green apples, she and I had many ponderous heart-to-hearts back when we were four or five.

"I'm gonna be a priest! Just like Mr. Burke."

"But Sophie!" I protested.

"It's what I'm supposed to be. I know it. I can feel it in my bones! I think in some funny sort of way I'm already a priest, and so are you."

"But Sophie, we're *girls*!" I insisted, wrinkling my brow and spitting out a seed for emphasis.

"So?" she queried.

The matter seemed simple to me, and closed. For Sophie Couch the matter was not closed. For her a matter was never closed or in any way definitive of who she was or who she might become. Sophie Couch was a young dreamer, a visionary, a child of far-reaching faith. Best of all, Sophie Couch was mine. She was my imaginary playmate, an extension of me, created to fill some of the relational gaps I experienced in being an only child for six years.

An imaginary playmate is a godsend. She is the raw matter out of which dreams are conceived, born, and nurtured into maturity. An imaginary playmate manifests a child's capacity to look beyond what seems to be and to come to know herself in other ways. Imagination is the stretching beyond what is apparent towards that which is concealed; the moving beyond what is towards that which might be.

> The apostles said to the Lord, "Increase our faith!" And the Lord said, "If you had faith as a grain of mustard seed, you could say to this sycamine tree, 'Be rooted up, and be planted in the sea,' and it would obey you."
>
> Luke 17:5–6

Imagination is the fabric out of which faith is cut—faith as a grain of mustard seed, the tiniest of seeds, the smallest faith. Not much at all, but some. And if you had it, look what you could do. You could say to the sycamine tree, the massive tree with the deepest roots, virtually impossible to uproot, "Be rooted up!" You could demand not only that it be uprooted, but also that it plant itself in the sea, where a tree could not possibly grow. And it would obey you.

Jesus was exaggerating. Faith is itself an exaggeration—an enlargement of what seems to be true, a bending of one's minds towards that which seems unreal.

Psychotherapists know how significant to healing the processes of dreams and fantasies are, the moving beyond what is conscious and under control into mysterious worlds of symbols, imagination, and chaos. This journey is crucial to a person's movement from brokenness or dysfunctional fear towards wholeness or what Tillich has called "the courage to be."

The faithful person will have an elastic mind, one that can bend without breaking. Jesus said, "Truly I say to you, whoever does not receive the kingdom of God like a child shall not enter it" (Luke 18:17). To this day I thank God for Sophie Couch, a sense of imagination that bent my mind beyond apparent parameters of reality and extended me into spaces that I have come since to know as equally real.

Faith is a process of being which embraces doubt. It has as much to do with play as with work, with laughter as with sobriety, with imagination as with concrete reality. In our work we are engaged in cleaning house, piloting planes, typing papers, counting stars. These activities are important to the extent that they nurture our faith. In our faith, we deal with relationship to self, God, others; relationship that we cannot work to produce, or earn, or resolve at Church conventions.

Faith is fundamentally incapable of articulation. It is a gracious process, a flow of being through us, by which we act not on the basis of what we know, or of what we can control, but rather on the basis of what we believe and of what controls us, which is to say, God, that inexpressibly good power which spirals through the universe, creating and recreating our being, our imagination, our faith.

Jesus worked on faith having no other goal than to live and grow in harmony with God. If we cannot fantasize beyond that which we can see and know to be real and possible, beyond that which we can work at and conceivably bring into being, then our faith is weak. In faith, Jesus went to Lazarus, and to the cross. In faith, Resurrection became reality.

A need for certainty is something we cultivate. We want to be sure of things. Ambiguity is hard to take. We want answers, not avoidances; yes or no, not maybe. It is easy to believe in that of which we can be sure. It is difficult to believe in that of which we cannot be sure. We have trouble embracing a faith in which there is room for doubt.

But doubt is as crucial to faith as darkness is to light. Without one, the other has no context and is meaningless. Faith is, by definition, uncertainty. It is full of doubt, steeped in risk. It is about matters not of the known, but of the unknown.

Certainty is a name for a territory that has been explored, mapped out, and staked. Faith is about that which is still unexplored, yet unmarked. We Episcopalians must decide whether or not we will continue to invest church law and polity with a degree of unbending certainty we have never been willing to invest in even the most compelling mandates of the Bible.

Faith is a process of leaping into the abyss not on the basis of any certainty about where we shall land, but rather on the belief that we *shall* land. We do not risk without some awareness that we are afraid to leap. Then leaping, we tremble towards integrity.

Faith is about the new, the mysterious, the surprising. Nobody has ever been there before. Nobody knows what it is. God, who is waiting there, calls us forth. Words and names adopt static, definitive connotations. Out of respect and fear, the people of Israel did not dare pronounce the holy name, the Tetragrammaton, the four initials "YHWH," which we have since spoken as "Yahweh," "Jehovah," "the Lord." It may be that our faith is diminished when we dare to utter God's name, let alone attempt to define, categorize, or theologize about that holy being which is moving and taking us into new, unknown places.

Idealism is an optimistic worldview in which human beings conceive of all good things as possible. If we work hard enough, gather enough knowledge, behave as we should, things will work out. Send money to the hungry, and they will be relieved. Pool human resources, and wars can be brought to an end. Educate Episcopalians, and they will accept the changes.

Liberal politics are grounded in idealism. Similarly, "humanism" incorporates an idealistic ethic whereby human will, human effort, and human consensus are seen to point to the solution of humankind's problems.

Idealism looks like faith. It is open to the future. It is often imaginative. It is built on concern about human beings. It is hopeful. But idealism is unlike faith in one significant way: for the idealist, human beings can transform the seemingly impossible into reality, much in the spirit of Don Quixote. We can seek, and we can realize, impossible dreams. For the faithful, we can do no more than we can do. The realization of impossible dreams is dependent upon the mysterious and elusive movement of God, in which we are employed in ways that we cannot imagine, let alone write into our political platforms.

This does not give us a mandate for political irresponsibility. For it is precisely the business of the faithful to work for the betterment of humankind and to dream impossible dreams in order that our visions for justice and peace be far-reaching enough to challenge and upgrade our work and our faith. But we had best know well that we are not finally in control of this world, this nation, this Church, or ourselves.

Faith as a grain of mustard seed—neither our work, nor our certainty, nor our idealism—will be that which brings us to our maturity as Christian people, faithful people, for whom the mind-bending magical possibility of an uprooted sycamine tree planted in the sea cannot be discarded offhandedly unless we can also discard all possibilities of mystery, grace, love, and surprises. Which is to say, all possibility of God.

> *Your visit showed me that you are fully and completely a minister of true Christian faith; Anglican faith. I am unsure what part your sex played in that reality, but we are not solely the bodies that encase us.... Your spiritual communion with us in the space in time we shared did provide a sanctuary for something far greater*

*than ourselves, as sexual beings or as individuals. God is truly not
dead. I am suddenly rather taken aback by these strong words I
have written. I believe they have been in stages of composition for
more time than I can know. The affirmation of faith is an incredible thing. It embraces positive energy, but I am now left trembling.*
—Letter to me from laywoman, Diocese of Albany, winter, 1975.

It was with my childhood playmate Elliott that I first became
aware of what I now would name *androgyny*, the interesting
blending of so-called "male" and "female" characteristics in all
people. At the time I had no name for this experience of myself
and my friend as children whose gender was neither asset nor
liability to our interests. We played with bride dolls and trucks.
We played cowgirl and house. We wore Lone Ranger T-
shirts with our mother's high heels. We scrapped and we cuddled. We were equally as at home in the kitchen helping our
mothers fix peanut butter sandwiches as we were in the creek
tiptoeing after crawfish. My relationship to Elliott gave me hope
that Sophie Couch's ruminations about life and vocation were
correct: perhaps I really *could* be myself when I grew up.

Hopefully and rather privately, I lived with my vocational
yearning to be ordained until I reached adolescence. A typical
teenager, I came crashing into those Dark Ages. It was hard to
lay aside my softball bat and try to be a "lady." It was traumatic
to exchange horseback riding for ballroom dancing. But I did,
for despite my parents' protestations, I had become convinced
by my social world that "to be a girl" was to be "cute." While
scaling the walls of the neighborhood school with my pal Tina
might strengthen my muscles, dancing school might make me
cute, a description that had never seemed to apply to me any
more than it did to Annie Oakley or Eleanor Roosevelt. Up until
then I had not cared. Suddenly I did.

I began to turn my back on the aspects of myself I considered
"unfeminine." One of the first to go were my fantasies about
being a priest. I began to think instead of wearing some hand-

some boy's monogram sweater. To bolster my female ego, nothing would do but that I catch and land only the most popular boys (read: sports stars). To have done so, which I did not, would have been confirmation of my cuteness or, if not that, of some teenage boy's peculiar capacity to transcend his own ego needs to meet mine.

Whether we are thirteen or fifty, "adolescence" is a time in our lives in which we battle with a monster. The monster is a loss of center, loss of self, loss of soul. "Soul" is an exceedingly deep, even primal, knowledge of being in relationship to God; of being a singular and significant thread in the fabulously complex, many dimensional, ever-expanding tapestry of an essentially good creative process. To lose one's soul is to be blocked off *not* from God's presence, but from *awareness* of God's presence and movement, both within and beyond oneself. To lose one's soul is to lose one's sense of the *authority* on which she lives.

The adolescence-monster bit me, as it will from time to time, but it did not destroy me. Sophie Couch would not let it. Discouraged that I could not be a homecoming queen or a cheerleader, I was nonetheless aware that I had a number of perfectly acceptable strong suits: scholarship, leadership, music and drama, and the Young Peoples' Service League (YPSL) at St. Martin's Episcopal Church in Charlotte, North Carolina.

I immersed myself in these endeavors, and I excelled. Moreover, I was happy. My days were spent doing homework; editing newspapers and yearbooks; cherishing Rodgers and Hammerstein; dancing in imitation of Mitzi Gaynor, *South Pacific*'s "Nellie Forbush"; and going to church, probably the strongest of these interests.

Perhaps I saw the Church as a refuge, a place to hide from societal pressures. Perhaps I saw it as a womb, a place to remain young and undeveloped. Perhaps I saw it as a home, a place to be myself. I think the Church was each of these to me and especially, at that time, a home, a place in which I could let my hair down and relax.

St. Martin's rector, Mr. Moore, was a gentleman in the tradition of South Carolina's thoroughly southern lower-coastal aristocracy—familial, soft-spoken, gracious in an innately pastoral way. His assistant, Mr. Forzly was an extroverted, bubbling, wonderfully witty man who both kept us in stitches and made each person feel important. Both men seemed unflappable. Upon one occasion, shortly after my confirmation, Mr. Forzly, calmly and in smooth rhythm, fished about in the chalice for my braces retainer which had slipped into the cup as I drank. His nonplussed manner of simply sliding it onto my raised palms, much in the likeness of a second wafer, spared me the mortification I was prepared to feel. Both priests liked me, and I knew it. Unlike school, in which competition was the key to both academic and extracurricular affirmation, my life in the Church seemed devoid of my having to prove anything to anyone.

Fran, Jane, and I were in the same grade. We were Episcopalians. We were as different as three white middle-class southern girls could be.

Fran was flirtatious and popular with boys. She was unusually artistic and bright. She adored nature, animals, and the out-of-doors. Her red hair, fiery disposition, and an occasional dreamy otherworldly quality made her seem at times to be an enigmatic pink angel, with a singular sense of self-determination.

Jane was a musical prodigy, a church organist at twelve, and —according to the adults—a genius. Jane was weird, and wonderful. She was a nonconformist in both interests and dress. She was socially retiring, and at anyone's party might well be found sitting at the piano in another room in communion with Chopin or Bach.

Most of the time Jane seemed to live in another world, one which she shared only with Fran and me. Her world was full of spirits and sacred things at war with demons. Jane was a sacramentalist and an Anglo-Catholic ("high church") complete with missal and rosary. To me, she was a holy person. I wondered occasionally if she had been born out of her time. Maybe all holy people seem to have been born out of their time.

We called ourselves the "Silly Scholars," and for all the giggly, wide-eyed hours we spent together, we might as well have been in heaven. One of our strongest, and most secretive, bonds was our common interest in the priesthood. For hours at a time, and for years, we discussed "the priesthood" as one might discuss "the Congo" or "rare plants."

But "issues" are of course born of human passion. They are empowered by the needs, desires, whims, and aspirations of human beings. This is as true for a theological issue, or doctrine, as it is for any other.

So it was that Fran, Jane, and I were not reflecting simply upon "the priesthood." We were talking about ourselves, and our longings. We were seeking and, by the grace of God, finding an exit from isolation into community.

The three of us tried to go to Holy Communion every day, partly to celebrate the holy communion among us all the time. One special day Fran, Jane and I found a coconut and celebrated communion with it in the side yard.

We began making our private Confessions on a somewhat regular basis, having requested that Mr. Moore, our hero and role model, hear us, even though St. Martin's was not a parish in which private Confession was the norm.

The night before my first Confession found me as nervous as I might have been the night before my wedding. Tediously, I tried to recall and record every "sin" I had ever committed and to guess the number of times I had committed it—like having "yelled at my mother eight hundred and forty-one times," having "lied fifty-two times," and having "sneaked into the school on weekends twice."

When the time came, Mr. Moore and I greeted each other and advanced awkwardly into the chancel. Facing the altar, a hardback chair sat immediately inside the sanctuary rail. Mr. Moore took his seat and I knelt weak-kneed behind him at the rail. "Bless me, Father, for I have sinned." One by one, I listed my sins. Fifteen or twenty minutes later, Mr. Moore said something to me about God's forgiveness, and then stood up, turned around, and smiled at me. His smile brought extraordinary relief. My quaking ceased suddenly, I held his eye, and I smiled cautiously back. Then I giggled and gaited confidently down the aisle and out the door into the laughter of Fran and Jane.

My second Confession was much briefer, since I had only to recount the "sins" of a several-week period. The private Confessions gradually subsided and finally ceased when I began to recognize the essence of Mr. Moore's smile in the expressions of Jane, Fran, Mama, Daddy, and other friends and strangers who conveyed to me an acceptance of who I am.

By the time we got to high school, Fran, Jane, and I had given up our semiconscious yearnings to be priests. As the pendulum swings by tension and pull, we swung back again into more realistic ruminations of what we might do upon graduation from college, the latter being a given. Fran talked about being a veternarian, a biologist, or an artist. Jane would be either a scientist or a musician. I wanted to be a teacher like Miss Smith.

Miss Smith was dynamic, sharp, aggressive. She knew history, and she knew how to teach it in such a way as to make students crave it. Moreover, she was single and, at the same time, seemed full and happy. Her energy was contagious. Here was a female who was strong and attractive, independent and warm, engaged in a profession she apparently enjoyed. In addition to everything else, Miss Smith was a communicant of St. Martin's. She was my ideal, my idol, my role model. Maybe, if I tried hard enough, I could grow up to be a teacher like Miss Smith.

Then, too, I might be a nun. Jane was considering entering a convent (which later she did enter, and leave). She and I talked incessantly about what this would mean and what type of Episcopal religious order we would want to join. Jane leaned towards the contemplative. I knew that I would fit better into a more physically active community, a teaching order perhaps.

I was beginning to think seriously about vocation. I wanted badly to blend my talents with a religious vocation of some form. Christian education offered a female vocation that did not appeal to me. Why, I cannot be sure. I had known one quite capable director of Christian education, but she was much older than I and the constellation of her role parameters had seemed fixed in such a way as to preclude my professional identification with her.

Like Miss Smith, I wanted to teach. Like a nun, I wanted to teach within the context of the Church. Like Mr. Moore, I wanted ... I was not sure what I wanted.

I could not find my vocational shoes on the feet of anyone I knew. I needed to find a vocation that would fit me. But where? Where could I go with the me that I knew best? What was I to do? I was confused.

People have different ways of reacting to the ecstatic and traumatic process of self-discovery and the internal conflicts precipitated by this process. Some people get depressed, others manic; some pop uppers, others downers; some batter their parents, others themselves; some flee into the ministry, others into marriage. Some people get migraines; I got nauseated.

I do not remember much about my senior year in high school. Memory is selective. I do remember that I spent a fair amount of time throwing up. Once again I was at work in academic, extra-curricular, dramatic, and ecclesiastical activities, discovering yet again my competencies. But I was experiencing increasingly these interests and skills as purposeless and painful.

So what if I had a goodly portion of brains, character, and charisma? So what if I were chairman [*sic*] of the Diocesan Youth Commission? So what if I were at my best immersed in Episcopal matters of youth work, liturgy, theology, and education? So what!

Then and there, at age seventeen, I felt myself nearing a dead-end, not because I was ready to give up these interests; not because I was tired and bored. I was approaching a dead-end in church vocation because, and only because, I was female. I was furious, but bottled up like a soda that has not yet been shaken so furiously as to explode, I lapsed into depression. During that year, my interest in the church all but disappeared.

*I feel that you and your associates are hurting the very church
that has already given so much of itself to you.*
                    —Letter to me from priest, Diocese of
                    North Carolina, summer, 1974.

I left for Randolph-Macon Woman's College, Lynchburg,
Virginia, in the fall of 1963. During my four years there, I
attended church from time to time, with only minimal feelings of
attachment, and absolutely no sense of commitment, to it.

At Randolph-Macon, I became interested academically in religion. The religion department was superb; the religion faculty,
affable and inspiring. Having stepped out of the Church, I
stepped into religious studies and spirituality, and found myself
immersed in matters that intrigued me.

Moreover, as the Church had once provided me with space to
be myself, Randolph-Macon became my home, offering me four
years of gracious opportunity to take myself seriously. In an all-
female student environment, the tasks to be done, jobs to be
filled, skills to be built, and vocational fantasies to be explored
became the business of women. For the moment, we could be the
editors, the scientists, the presidents, the artists, the varsity
sportspeople, and the ministers, without any fear of perversely
trespassing on the turf of "male ego." Here, at last, was a place
for our own ego-building; here, at last, a vocational heaven. And
I gloried in it.

At the encouragement of a college friend, I spent the summer
of 1965, between sophomore and junior years, as a teacher's
aide in a remedial second- and third-grade class at the Henry
Street Settlement House on New York City's Lower East Side.
Something significant happened to me that summer. I am still not
sure what it was. Maybe it was the impact of New York City—its
beauty and its terror. Maybe it was the stimulation, and inspiration, of the people with whom I worked. Maybe it was my journey to what was, for me, like a foreign land, far away from
everything I had ever known. For whatever reasons, this was a
sacramental summer, in which every conversation, action, color,

smell, sound, sight, value, touch, and emotion seemed to point towards some deeper level of reality—within me and around me. I felt small, and open. I felt free, as if my being were itself a sacrament, an outward sign of grace. It was as if I had worked my way out of a nineteen-year-old cocoon and was balanced at the edge of a twig trying to decide whether or not to fly.

As children mastered "double Dutch" jump rope with amazing agility and parents talked about the cost of living with alarm; as Norman Thomas spoke to us about socialism, and Barbra Streisand sang to us that no one would rain on her parade; and as my colleagues and I weathered a water shortage on the streets of New York, something happened in me. I began to think beyond Randolph-Macon's "red brick wall" towards the shaping of values on which I could act. I returned to college and resigned from the school's prestigious "secret societies," to which I had been elected the previous year. I left them because they were, for me, a sign of the spoils, the competition and clamor predicated by a need to prove something to someone.

I write in retrospect, of course. Upon my resignation, I held up "ideology" as my reason for taking this action. The issue, I was careful to point out, was social justice. I did not believe that organizations which were closed and exclusive and existed, insofar as I could tell, primarily to extol themselves were helpful in the creation of community spirit.

I believed this then. I believe it now. But it was important for me to gradually make the connection between the ideology and my own experiences. It was important for me to come to realize that such ideas had not been simply handed to me—by Norman Thomas, Karl Marx, Dorothy Day, or for that matter, Jesus of Nazareth. The "ideology" was, in fact, *my belief*, and my belief had grown out of *my own life processes* which had included the experience of exclusion: my black maid's exclusion from our dining-room table; my exclusion from her house, the sixth-grade baseball team, the eighth-grade sock-hop, the acolytes' group, and the possibility of ordination in the Episcopal Church.

The capacity to act on a belief—to resign from the secret societies, to join resistance to an outrageous war, to take small steps towards Philadelphia and come what may—is grounded in a gracious sense of freedom, such as that which I had felt stirring within me on Henry Street. It is the Sophie Couch in each person, the soulful, imaginative knowledge of oneself and others as commonly unique reflections of something that is basically good, something that is God. In its movement, its image, its spirit, we are called to go with it wherever it goes.

One may be shot down, put down, or ignored, and she is still able to laugh. For the movement rolls on, and with this holy process, she herself is able to roll with the punches. In the words of the Church Militant, "the victory is won."

> *In these moments of decision, we are indeed fortunate that we have all of you who walk where we have not. Your enthusiasm and commitment will help to make us all strong.*
> —Letter to me from laywoman,
> Diocese of Massachusetts, fall, 1974.

I wanted to continue my studies in religion after graduation from college. With the encouragement of my major professors, I decided to go to Seminary. I chose Union Theological Seminary in New York City both because it was in "The City" and on the basis of its long-standing reputation as an excellent interdenominational school. I had no more than a fuzzy vocational notion of what I might "do" with a seminary education.

For four years I had been all but peripherally uninvolved in the Church. Here at Union, for the first time in my life, I met women of many denominations who were talking about ordination and actively seeking it. I was astonished. I did not know how I felt about women being ordained deacons, priests, and bishops in the Episcopal Church. Faith and common sense assured me that there were no reasons why women should be excluded from Holy Orders. But I had concluded somewhere along the way that *I* did not want to be ordained, and I could not understand why *any* woman would want to be.

A nauseous sensation gripped my gut every time I set foot in the Episcopal parish to which I had been assigned for my seminary field work. I felt as if I did not belong there. The Church was no longer my home, a place in which I could be myself, a place in which I could give creatively from the core of my being. To have been myself, immersing myself in those endeavors which could spring from my center, I would have been acting too much like a priest, a male seminarian, a man. I was furious at the Church, but as in the past, I could not reveal my anger, or even experience it in a sustained, constructive way. Hence, I was lethargic, quiet, depressed. I did not know what this meant. I did know that something was the matter.

My field work colleague, Bob, must have known that I wanted to be ordained. I was even able to say so, couching my wish in terms of conjecture, "If I were a man, I would be . . ." I did not want to be a man; I wanted to be a priest. The Church, on the basis of a strand of catholic tradition which in turn is rooted in a fear of women, had equated the two: PRIEST = MAN.

For a woman, the PRIEST = MAN equation is a Catch 22: She is likely to be a strong, aggressive person to be seeking ordination to the priesthood at this time, given the opposition with which she must contend. Hence, she is perceived by some to be "acting like a man." Given her tenacity, it is likely she would have been welcomed long ago by ecclesiastical authorities if she were male. However, left standing on the boundaries of acceptability, if not completely outside, she infers that only "real women," if any at all, can be ordained priests. And yet if she were behaving like a "real woman" (compliant, undemanding, sweet), she would not be a likely aspirant to a vocation in which women cannot long manifest "sugar and spice and everything nice."

In Massachusetts, a priest said to me recently, "I want women priests to be real women, not to cut their hair short and wear pants." Gritting his teeth and smiling simultaneously, he spoke to me as I stood before him in my blue summer slacks and with my hair barely reaching the center of my neck. "By the way, I wasn't referring to you!" he added hurriedly.

"Oh?"

In North Carolina, a priest said to me several years ago, "I really can't stand to see some of the women deacons running around in short skirts. How do you girls expect us fellows to be able to concentrate on the Lord!"

I looked at him and wondered how much time he spent concentrating on the Lord.

During my first year at Union, I had begun to be barely conscious of the vocational and sexual snares in which we women were caught. Not only was vocational calling creeping into my consciousness, and confusing me, my sexuality was also beginning to surface. I was wet behind the ears sexually, an innocence I had tediously nurtured not as much out of self-respect as out of fear. I had not known what to make of the strange, exciting, stirring flow within myself that seemed to propel me simultaneously outward toward others, and inward toward my own soul.

I believe that the sexual flow within us is sacred, a manifestation of spiritual movement. It offers the possibility of that which we name as "good" and that which we name as "evil." Creative and destructive, unifying and alienating, sexuality is a sign of the power moving through us and all creation, the holy being, God, who moves bearing life and death in a strangely conjunctive way. To realize such power within one's own body—oneself—and to cultivate a capacity to move with this sexuality in a joyful, responsible way is both freeing and frightening. Terrified by sex, I had chosen to pretend for twenty-two years that it had nothing to do with me.

At seminary, I experienced myself as coming alive to sexual feelings in a way I had never known. It seemed as if I were "turned on" to everybody about whom I had any warm feelings.

Within myself, I was aware of a surging energy that ached to carry me passionately both toward the core of my being and into the created world of marvelous people around me. "Horny" would be too flip a word. I yearned to embrace and be embraced. I longed to come alive in relationship to myself, others, and the gift of life we shared. I had never been healthier, and it scared me, spiraling me to the edge of sanity.

Fearful of my sexuality, depressed about myself in general and my vocation in particular, I plunged into my own private space and took refuge behind walls I had constructed to protect me from myself. It was in this fall of my first year at Union, 1967, that I began to make a long journey downward. A going down, and a reaching up; a movement into hell toward a discovery of myself as integral to the movement of God.

Bev Harrison, at the time dean of women students at Union, responded to me as if I not only mattered, but were moreover a person of some very real significance—to her and to others. While I felt myself paralyzed by fear and confusion—I would not study, play, laugh, socialize—Bev was gentle, consistent, and imperative in her persuasions. She told me I could make it. Bev, not I, was aware that the crux of my so-called "problems" was my stubborn refusal to accept the socially and ecclesiastically defined role-parameters of my gender. She, not I, was aware that *my only authentic problem lay in my agonized belief that I had a problem.* Bev Harrison's gift to me was her standing back and letting me go under alone so that I might come to know, splashing about in the swamps of my own self-doubt, that I would have to save myself or drown. Bev and others could offer me encouragement. Only I could make the decision to live, and to live creatively.

And so, I went under, sinking into swirling currents of rage, directed against myself rather than against the conditions in Church and society which had bottled me up. Into deeper depression; into futile attempts at manipulating those around me to take responsibility for my salvation; into despair. Weeks. Months. I could not stand the pain of the loneliness and the confusion. I could not tolerate this feeling of helplessness, and I could not lay claim to an autonomous strength, ours by grace, with which I could help myself. I could not seem to pick myself up and walk, as Jesus had commanded those who asked him for help.

My roommate, Jean, was frightened by my catatonic brooding. Moreover, she was annoyed. She was able to see that I was only heaping grief upon myself; that I was indeed my own worst enemy. For I could not be gentle with myself. I battered myself relentlessly.

Eventually the Church would pick up this battering and take the lash to us. Although painful, the Church's reaction to our ordinations was predictable. I could have expected nothing other. For I had learned that such frenzied madness leveled against people who are trying to move in harmony with the Spirit cannot be avoided; and that it is furious, futile clamor. I could only look with some pity, and much purposeful annoyance, on the Episcopal Church's "confusion" about us, much as I could see myself seven years earlier as having been a pitiful soul in need of a caring kick-in-the-can to get up and get with it.

I began to get with it. People who are concerned about their psyches often study psychology as if it were going out of style, and people who are concerned about their souls often turn to the Bible and theology. I began to read Freud, Jung, Psalms, Jeremiah, Romans, Bonhoeffer, Tillich, Charles Williams.

During college, I had read several of Charles Williams' novels. I went back to pick up where I had left off. Upon occasion, one will read a book or come upon a work of art which speaks so deeply to her own soul that she feels almost as if the work were her own. This is, I think, an uncommon reaction, unique and personal; it has been my reaction to the works of Charles Williams.

In his last and most intricately constructed novel,[3] Williams develops the character of Pauline Anstruther, a young woman who lives in dread of meeting herself. Pauline is terrified. She knows that the meeting will occur. She does not know whether it will enhance her life or insure her death—or both. She knows only that she cannot continue to evade this communion of selves.

The novel's several themes are interwoven to culminate in Pauline's reunion with her *Doppelgänger*, an event that is both terrible and unspeakably good.

God is, for Williams, not an evil God; nor simply a good God. God is a "Terrible Good," a power so extraordinary as to incorporate mysteriously, sacramentally, all that we have come to name as either "good" or "evil."

As I reread *Descent into Hell*, I knew that Pauline Anstruther was, in some sacramental way, Carter Heyward. I knew the terror within myself and within the movement of God. And I had some sense of the good within. The God that I knew was indeed a "Terrible Good." Slowly, I began to recognize my confusion and conflicts as integral to whatever creativity, courage, or vocation I had.

> And he said to all, "If any one would come after me, let her deny herself and take up her cross daily and follow me. For whoever would save her life will lose it; and whoever loses her life for my sake, she will save it."
>
> Luke 9:23–24 AUTHOR'S PARAPHRASE

At the center of Christian faith is a curious paradox: if we are to save our lives, we must lose them. If we are to live as whole people, we must be broken. If we are to know peace, we must enter into conflict. If we are to be certain about anything, we must be able to celebrate the ambiguities within us and around us. If we are to ascend into heaven, we must descend into hell.

For years, I envisioned losing and finding one's life as being not only distinctly separate experiences, but also as best accessible to me in chronological order: I must first live in doubt and conflict. I might later grow into faith and peace. Metaphorically, I must first be crucified; I might someday know the glory of the resurrection.

Gradually, I began to realize that life does not exist for me somewhere further down the pike. We do not become whole people, saved people, peaceful people the day we finish therapy, give our lives to Christ, get married, get ordained, or set ourselves in some new direction. Again and again we are aware of our wholeness and our salvation when we are able to face and enter into the brokenness and confusion within us, between us in relationship, and around us in the world.

In paradox the contradictions are concurrent. We do not lose life today and "win" it tomorrow, as a reward for having died. The losing and the finding are a single process, a single reality. I live and I die simultaneously. I am faithful and doubtful at the same time. If I know who I am today, and I do, it is in the knowing of myself as a person who, like anyone, does not know much at all about who she is.

Awareness of paradox—contradiction, confusion, and wisdom —at the heart of things is fundamental to awareness of *sacrament*: what we feel, or see, or touch, or eat is only one aspect of what really is. The bread is more than bread; it is body. It is more than body; it is a peace that we cannot understand. It is more than peace; it is our unity. It is more than unity; it is God. It is not only a transcendent Being; it is God-in-us. It is not only God-in-you-and-me; it is God-in-all. It is not only God-in-all-people; it is God-in-all-creation, God-in-wheat-and-rain-sun. It is God-in-bread.

Like bread, each of us is a sacrament, an outward and visible sign of an inward and spiritual grace. We manifest many signs of grace, and signs of much terror as well. What we see each time we look at ourselves is only some aspect of who we are.

Feeling weak and wobbly, I began to think paradoxically of standing up and walking. The support I received from people at Union Seminary this first year was empowering. They could not do what I needed to do for myself. They could, however, stand alongside and care. In their presence, the terror seemed to subside and I could begin to realize the holiness of many moments. These people were my priests. From them I learned something about my own vocation, a priestly commitment to sacrament— the hiddenness of God, a Terrible Good, in all reality.

Rarely have I met a person with such power in conveying the Spirit of God, and of priesthood, with such integrity. And for the first time in my experience such a priest is also a woman/feminist. I want you to know how grateful I am. Only occasionally any more does worship inspire me to the point that I feel really good about being a woman in ministry in this time in history! You affirmed me and called me into the risk and hope of tomorrow.
　　　　　　　—Letter to me from United Methodist minister,
　　　　　　　Atlanta, Georgia, Winter, 1975.

After a year at Union, complete with the instructive experience of the spring rioting at our neighbor Columbia University, I withdrew from seminary and returned to work at St. Martin's in North Carolina. Over Easter vacation, I had met David, a young Australian priest who had joined St. Martin's staff as curate. Not only was he charming; he was immersed in the very ministries that were attractive to me—liturgy, teaching, counseling, community and youth work. Our interests seemed synonymous —peace movement, race relations, working in support of Robert Kennedy's presidential campaign (1968), folk and rock music, art, drama, the out-of-doors, and a special affinity for any movie, book or conversation that related to our common sacramental view of reality. David and I were soul mates, feeling as if we had been born together, sometimes it seemed in another world. From the beginning, we were almost inseparable.

At the time, David was opposed to women's ordination much in the spirit and jargon of many of our present hard-core opponents who believe that a male priesthood is fundamental to a divine schema. Although I had no conscious inclination to seek ordination myself, I found myself standing in unambiguous opposition to David's position. The more we argued about this "hypothesis," the more uneasy I became. Somewhere inside I knew that we were not talking simply about "women's ordination." We were discussing *our* relationship—whether or not I myself intended to be ordained. I grew to both love and hate this man and the charm, charisma, and comfort of the implications he laid before me regarding his role as the head and mine as the helpmate. I wanted both to follow him and to run in the opposite direction. His feelings about me were equally as ambivalent, I was to learn.

Late one spring day in 1969, as David and I drove back to the church from an afternoon of hospital visiting, we talked about where we saw ourselves headed in our relationship. I felt ready to go with him back to Australia and said so. He had other feelings:

"Carter, I think you're trying with your whole heart—lovingly, enthusiastically, skillfully—to live out the vocation *you* seek through *my* vocation. Sometimes I get the feeling that you want to *be* me. I must say to you that I think you'd be a burden to me, or to any priest you were to marry, because your identity is too wrapped up in the priesthood. You're trying to hang onto something you can't have."

I asked him to stop the car and let me out. Without further conversation, I got out, walked back to the church, and that night, fell apart. I was devastated. Several days later, I left Charlotte on a trip to visit old college and seminary friends along the East Coast. I spent two weeks back at Union Seminary, discussing my situation with former classmates and professors, among whom there seemed to be an unspoken consensus: I should consider returning to seminary to pursue my *own* ministerial vocation.

Several weeks later when I returned to Charlotte, David was packing to leave for Australia. I saw him only once before he left. He looked as white as a ghost as he bade me farewell, and I recall standing expressionless and silent before him. He had become a symbol of pain to me. I was unsure what the pain was about, but I experienced it as wrenching and thoroughgoing, and I had no words for it.

Fortunately, and to my surprise, the church work in which I had been involved professionally for nine months was dependent upon neither David's presence nor his love. In the course of my work as St. Martin's parish assistant, I had begun to emerge unwittingly and almost unconsciously into a sense of my own vocation. I worked well at St. Martin's and loved it. I did not yet know what this meant, but the questions were surfacing, and an active, intentional search for my vocation was on.

On a gamble that I might find something I was looking for there, I reapplied to Union Seminary, finished my work at St. Martin's, took an interim position in the Model Cities program in Charlotte's public school system, and returned to Union in the fall of 1970. As was timely enough for me, the General Convention of the Episcopal Church opened the *diaconate*—order of deacons, first of the three orders of ordained ministry (deacon, priest, bishop)—to women "on the same basis as men" that same fall.[4]

Although I did not expect it, the time was at hand. If my first year at seminary had been marked by trauma, this second year was graced by rapid growth which I myself could feel even as it set in.

I can attribute this growth to two simultaneous and complementary processes in my life at the time: *psychotherapy* and a *women's consciousness-raising group*, from both of which I initially shied away, and each of which landed me near the heart of Christian faith: a realization of my own being's movement in harmony with that of the Holy Spirit.

The Carter-David dynamics had suggested to me that therapy might be helpful. Soon into the 1970–71 school year, I managed to swallow some of my anxieties about therapy and enter it. My therapist, Bob, was a young man, about David's age, a pastoral counselor. I visited him each week, discovering as months wore on that this person both challenged me at the core of my being, fantasies, and fears; and supported me in what were some very painful growth processes. Slowly, I began to look forward to our sessions together.

Alongside, my closest Union friends, Jean and Linda, had urged me, time and again, to join them in the formation of a women's consciousness-raising group, in which we would reflect together on being female. At first, resistant to anything that seemed to ring of "women's lib," I had insisted that I did not need such a group. Several months into the year, I decided to give it a try, primarily for the companionship it might offer.

In therapy, I began to recall times, places, and processes in which I had rather passively attached myself to some person and attempted to live my life through him or her. I began to wonder where my determination to assert myself had gone.

In consciousness-raising, I began to remember Sophie Couch —the determinative, self-assertive me.

In therapy, I began to talk about my own vocational goals, including ordination, which I had denied for so long, even to myself.

In consciousness-raising, I began to hear other women discussing similar vocational aspirations and similar denial.

In therapy, I began to view myself as a potent individual; and as I had always viewed other people, a person very human and worthy of tenderness.

In consciousness-raising, I began to experience community. I began to realize that I was not alone.

In therapy, I began to see myself as victimized—by Church, society, and most surely, by myself. My rage began to surface.

In consciousness-raising, I began to feel strong, and hopeful— or, at least, on my way.

At the same time, across the Pacific, David too was growing. He was attempting to discover more about his own vocation and his own relationships to people like me—to me in particular. About a year after our separation, he and I began corresponding.

He wrote of his new parish and friends in Melbourne. I told him about my decision to return to Union, my therapy, my consciousness-raising group. I told him that I believed *myself* called to the priesthood. He made no response to the latter, and continued to write me, with increasing frequency, about his parish work; his warm, confused feelings about me; his own internal growth processes—both invigorating and frightening to him. I

shared with him much of my own inner struggling including my
ambivalent feelings about him. As months passed, he and I once
again became close—this time at a distance of thousands of
miles. Both of us agreed that it would help to see each other
again.

Toward the end of my first year in therapy and consciousness-
raising, David suggested that I come for a couple of years to
visit him in Australia. As if spiraled backward despite myself, I
found myself thinking in terms of actually going. I would put my
own ordination on the back burner for awhile.

The women in my consciousness-raising group were astonished at my serious discussion of this trip. My therapist Bob
withheld all spoken judgment and simply listened each week as I
presented my plans to him.

I was eager to see David. I wanted to go. At the same time,
something was the matter. My decision did not set right with me.
I found myself swinging back and forth:

Yes, I wanted to see David.
Yes, I wanted to be ordained.

The former would entail a gamble, a risk—for neither David
nor I could have any idea of whether our relationship would
"work out" for two days, let alone two years.

The latter, too—ordination—would involve risking. I would
be risking not only rejection from bishops, parishes, and denomination, on the basis of my gender (for I believed that my gender
was the only conceivable impediment to my acceptance as a
candidate for ordination). I would be risking my self-image as
well, stepping into a space in which I would most surely be
charged with all manner and means of "unfeminine sins" against
the "masculine ego," on whose turf I would be seen as trespassing. I would be risking good feelings about myself. I would be
risking an entry into loneliness.

*It was in that spring of 1971 that I chose to apply for ordina-
tion.* The time had come for me to concentrate on *my own*

vocational goals. Furthermore, I must have known that I could not enter creatively into relationship with someone else unless I were involved in creative relationship with myself.

I wrote David of my plans. He was disappointed, and yet affirmative of me. He wrote back that he wished we could have made an attempt to work things out, but that he did believe my decision was right—for me, and definitely for the Church itself. He noted that he was still unclear about women and the priesthood, but that he would continue to think and pray over the matter.

Happily and hopefully—with the unconcealed delight and support of my therapist, my North Carolina parish leaders, and my seminary friends and faculty—I made official application for ordination to the bishop of my home diocese. I felt honest, purposeful, clear about what I was doing. I also felt scared, for it was so new.

In July, 1971, I received word from the bishop. His response to me was "No, not at this time." In August, I visited him to find out why I had been rejected and was told that I was confused.

"In what specific ways?" I asked.

He said he didn't know exactly but he had the impression that I was kind of helter-skelter.

Being rejected in my application for ordination in North Carolina was a blow to me for I had always considered North Carolina my home. It was there that I had longed to live out my vocation. The ethos, the people, the ways of the state were my own. I was unhappy to realize that I would have to grow further away from my birth-roots if I intended to move with God towards a vocation to which I believed myself directed. But Christian vocation is seldom what, or where, we expect it to be. When Jesus said, "Follow me," this call ordinarily involved his disciples' departures from places, people, and occupations with which they had been at home.

Furthermore, the bishop's rejection of me on the grounds of "confusion" about which he could not, or would not, elaborate initially hurt—and confused!—me.

Of course I was confused. What woman in her right mind would not be confused if she felt herself drawn—by faith, talent, and with strong parish and seminary support—towards ordination in a Church in which her gender made her, at best, a curiosity piece and, at worst, an abnormal intruder into male space?

But, on the other hand, I was bound to wonder . . . "Maybe I *am* mixed up, wrong." The decision not to join David exacerbated my self-doubt.

The most insidious demon against which we women have to contend is the human inclination to swallow and digest what is said about us.

We begin to reclaim our souls when we are able to cast out this demon of self-doubt and move on—angrily, caringly, emphatically—in a knowledge that we have been violated, not because we are "confused," "aggressive," "sick," or "incompetent," but rather because we are people who are attempting to live fully our potential.

In a society and a Church in which woman has been put into a place out of which she cannot move, any effort on her part to burst out of this place will be considered strange or abnormal. Those invested with institutional authority are likely to get their backs up and balk defensively at her efforts. For such a woman is a threat to both men and women who have heavy investment in maintaining the present order.

And the threat is not imaginary. It is real. As women enter into new ecclesiastical roles, with responsibilities not only for decision making and leadership in heretofore male arenas of activity, but also for new *symbol-building*, the present order *will* change. All roles, those of both men and women, will change. Nothing will remain the same. We are agents of transformation.

Our transforming power is not inherent to our gender, for we are simply human, like our brothers. Our power lies in our having been born, nurtured, and acculturated into a corporate symbol: a symbol not necessarily of "femininity," but rather a symbol of *difference*. Together, we offer a difference to the

Church, a difference that includes the corporate experience of exclusion, and the particular experiences of being daughter, wife, mother, lover, and the various other roles we have played.

I do not offer any peculiar brand of "softness" or "sweetness," "seductiveness" or "saintliness" to the Episcopal Church. I offer myself—my softness, my toughness, my sweetness, my bitterness, my seductiveness, my honesty, my saintliness, and my sinfulness of the Church. As a woman, together with my sisters, I offer a difference—a different ethic, derived from collective exclusion, which I will help build on behalf of other "outsiders"; a different visual, audible, sensory image I will help create; a different theology I will help shape; a different priesthood into which I have been ordained; indeed, a different Episcopal Church, as one manifestation of catholic Christendom.

People seem amazed that so much turmoil has spun off the Philadelphia ordinations. But why? The Church is in throes of rebirth. An old order is passing away. The process of renewal is always denied by a few, resisted by many, unwelcomed by most, and chaotic to all.

The wisest among us will move with the currents of the chaos, not resisting them, but rather letting ourselves be washed in time onto new shores. We will not recognize the shores, but they will be our home. We can be then amazed appropriately by God's capacity for recreation and offering of new life to us, God's confused people.

> *You have planted many seeds, given us all much hope and great joy. I pray your efforts will be blessed by success and that it will not change you. For my part, I promise to nourish those seeds within my reach.*
>
> —Letter to me from laywoman,
> Diocese of Long Island, fall, 1974.

Attending an interdenominational seminary was educational in the exposure it offered me to the diversity of experiences and symbols within Judaeo-Christian tradition.

At Union I was able to begin consciously shaping my theology not as *apart from* the Anglican tradition, but rather as Anglican *within a larger ecumenical tradition.*

Moreover, at Union, in my own experiential contexts of therapy, consciousness-raising, prayer, conversation, reading, work, growth, I began to take heart, to have faith, to feel empowered. From this position of faithful strength, I began to better understand and articulate my identity. In so doing, I began to better understand and articulate the meaning of "priesthood":[5]

All human beings are people of God.

For Christians, the sign of this reality is baptism, by which a person acknowledges (or has acknowledged for her) her being as a person of God.

All baptized people are priests, comprising "a priesthood of believers," which is the Christian Church. Fundamental to the Church are its faith, its community, its inclusiveness, and its mission.

Faith is personal investment in God's presence and God's transcendence. It has to do with caring about God and with awareness of God. Faith is well sustained by what German theologian Dorothee Sölle calls *"phantasie"*[6] and by what I have termed "imagination": the capacity to bend one's mind beyond what seems to be the case and to see beyond what is visible to the eye.

Community (koinonia) is when two or three are gathered together in faith. A common language (such as creed, prayer book, catechism) is helpful, but not mandatory, for community. Sacramental awareness of reality—or awareness of hidden, "invisible," layers of reality—is vital for community and enables the community to stretch its imagination, in faith, beyond its own physical parameters to include people, processes, and events from other places and times.

Inclusiveness is that characteristic of extension beyond present boundaries, in order that community can grow, change, and remain always open to new possibilities. Inclusiveness is usually strange and frightening for members of the community. But *ex*clusiveness, which purposes to limit community within fixed parameters, is deadly. A community cannot live long unless it changes and grows. And community will not grow and change unless it assumes that "outsiders" have as much to offer the community as the community has to offer them.

Mission is that to which the faithful and inclusive Christian community is called. There are many biblical mandates for mission: among them are Matthew 25:31–46, in which we are told to feed the hungry, welcome the stranger, clothe the naked; Mark 12:29–31, in which we are told that we are to love the Lord our God, and our neighbor as ourself; "The Beatitudes" as recorded in Matthew and Luke. These are only a few of many passages of mandate in Scripture. We are always selective in the ones we choose.

The fundamental mission of the Church is to bring people to faith. Taken as a whole, the Holy Scriptures make plain this mission: we are to bring people to faith by action in faith towards people. By its very nature, faith brings people to a peace they, and we, cannot understand; and by its very nature, faith consistently undergirds a strong ethic of awareness, concern, and involvement in matters of human justice, human freedom, and human dignity. For, in faith, all people are seen for what they are: people of God, no more and no less than I myself.

All Christian people are called by God to this priestly and inclusive community of faith and mission. This community needs people within it whose primary investment of energy and time will be to the sustenance of the community's faith and mission. The community will call forth such people from within it to be its "priests."

These members of the community will be called forth for "ordination" as priests. These people will have skills and interests that will be focused specifically on the facilitation of the Church's growth in faith, community, inclusiveness, and mission. These people need to be "sacramental functionaries," which is to say, they need to have a functional sacramental eye for how it is that faith, community, inclusiveness, and mission are interlocked —often invisibly—and held actively in creative tension.

The ordained priest has one primary task: to help maintain the faithfulness of the community.

As a Lecturer at Union Theological Seminary in New York City, Carter Heyward participates in a discussion of "theological imagery," Spring, 1975.

The ordained priest is self-consciously a sacramental person, acutely aware of many layers comprising a single reality.

The ordained priest is, in faith, a person of prayer—of phantasie and imagination.

The ordained priest is a member of community. Within it, he can be himself. From it, he derives strength.

The ordained priest is an inclusive person. She is actively aware of the functional and ethical imperatives for inclusion of people in community—regardless of color, religion, age, state of health, nationality, ethnicity, class, gender, sexuality.

The ordained priest is a missioner. He is nonapologetic for his mission. He is prophetic, pastoral, liturgical, instructive, enabling, leading, following; he had best be able to cope with ambiguity and to embrace the unknown and unexpected.

The ordained priest is her vocation. For her, there is no demarcation between the person and the mission, no bifurcation between who one is and what one does. She *is* what she thinks, feels, knows, believes, says, and does.

The ordained priest is a priest forever. "Priesthood" is not a coat he can take off and leave behind at the office. Functional, it is—like any function, carved out in the person's character. Etched upon his soul. "One cannot go home again." A retired doctor is still a doctor in terms of skills, interests, values, essential vocation. Similarly, a retired, removed, or deposed priest is still a priest. Ordination is thoroughgoing and indelible.

The ordained priest is simply human. She shares the same needs, fears, confusions, problems. She is a member of the same humanity.

The ordained priest is called to a life of holiness. To live a holy life is to live a simply human life, in faith.

I realize that nowhere in the preceding reflections do I mention, explicitly, "Jesus Christ." Throughout the reflections, Jesus Christ has been close at hand, and is written implicitly between each line. Perhaps another task of the priest is to make explicit what is implicit—to point to Jesus Christ's presence everywhere; and to make implicit what is explicit—that is to demythologize and humanize what is, at best, the meaningful language of a common faith; and what is at worst, ecclesiastical rhetoric.

My participation in ordained priesthood is not something that I can separate from my involvement in the diaconate and in the priesthood of all believers. My baptism, similarly, is not something that separates me from nonbaptized persons. Simone Weil was a mystic philosopher who, *because* she believed in Christ Jesus, refused to be baptized. I understand this. I pray for the day when the people of God will have obliterated barriers: not only between women and men, Catholic and Protestant, clergy and laity, but also between Christians and non-Christians. When, in fact, all people are *assumed* to be the people of God; when baptism is a sign of inclusion of the Church in the world, and not of the exclusion of the Church from the world. When it becomes superfluous to "talk about" Jesus Christ—as it will be when women and men are so fully aware of God's presence within, between and among us that Jesus Christ is being lived out rather than talked out. Each person will be doing, and being, and living Jesus Christ. There will be nothing more to say. We will have discovered the laughter at the heart of things.

> *Are you hooked by clericalism? Are you hooked by wanting power? Are you into wanting to be a priest so that you can change the overload of clerical influence, or do you just want your share of it? Up until now I haven't heard any statements from any of you that sound as if you are out for anything but your share of the action.*
>
> —Letter to me from laywoman,
> Diocese of New York, fall, 1974.

Many of us have chosen to grow as creatively, charitably, and critically as we can where we have our roots—as long as we can, with integrity. And we have our ecclesiastical roots in the Episcopal Church. Inherent in its present structure is a threefold order of ordained ministries, which—despite idealistic protestations to the contrary—remains a hierarchical arrangement or "chain of command" from top to bottom. Bishops are on top; then priests; then deacons. And laypeople? Sometimes it seems as if laypeople exist so that clergy can find self-esteem and grow in faith, rather than all Christians—laity and clergy—existing so that all people might find self-esteem and grow in faith.

I take great comfort, and find inspiration, in the fact that Jesus did not hate or leave his religious tradition, but rather loved it and worked to restore it to its soul—its awareness of God's active presence. Where it was errant, Jesus challenged it, often harshly. Where it made ungodly, compromising demands upon him, Jesus ignored it and went about his business, together with his disciples.

It is ironic, though understandable in terms of sin, that just as Jesus, a Jew, found himself in confrontation with Judaism, we Christians today find ourselves confronting Christianity.

With this general condition as backdrop to current Episcopal affairs, the reader should recognize certain specific Episcopal conditions in order more fully to grasp that context of the events that have transpired.

Male or female, a person must be ordained a "deacon" for at least six months prior to his or her ordination as a "priest." In the biblical tradition of Stephen, a deacon is a "server." The diaconate, or order of deacons, is the *fundamental* order of ordained ministry in the catholic tradition to which the Episcopal Church adheres. The diaconate is that order upon which the other two orders—priesthood and episcopate—rest. A person does not graduate from the diaconate. A priest or a bishop is still a deacon—a servant to the world. In order to be a good priest or bishop, the person must be a good deacon, one who sees *service* as fundamental to ministry.

The second of the orders, priesthood, is the *common* order of ordained ministry in the catholic tradition. I used the word "common" to mean usual, ordinary, that which is to be expected. When an Episcopalian enters the ordained ministry, it is commonly expected that she or he will be ordained a priest. Priesthood is the "sacramental" order of ministry. The priest is that person ordained to administer sacraments, as well as to teach and preach a sacramental faith within the community of believers—which is to say, a faith in the unseen or invisible presence of God in all reality: in birth, life, death; in all events and processes. Since the Episcopal Church is one in which sacrament is central to both its theology and its liturgy, those who purpose to commit themselves professionally to the sustenance of the Church's theology and worship must be sacramentalists.

The third order of ordained ministry is the episcopate, the order of bishops, or "overseers," in the tradition of Peter and the other apostles, those commissioned by God to be chief pastors— "pastors to the pastors," "priests to the priests." A bishop is elected from among priests to serve as the head of a "diocese" (large cluster of parishes; often about half the size of a state). There are at present over one hundred dioceses in the Episcopal Church and over two hundred bishops, some dioceses having more than one, and some bishops being retired or resigned from official diocesan responsibilities.

When a person is ordained a deacon, the expectation is *commonly* that he or she will be ordained a priest.[7] All along, she or he has been seeking ordination to the priesthood. The new deacon has understood this. The bishop has understood this. This mutual expecation regarding the deacon's future ordination to the priesthood is in fact that upon which his or her ordination to the diaconate has been based.

As a deacon, the man or woman is allowed to baptize, officiate at weddings and funerals, preach, and minister to congregations and other groups as the bishop's and priest's assistant. She, or he, is *not* allowed to serve as rector (official head) of a parish, pronounce God's blessing or absolution from sin, or serve as celebrant of Holy Communion, the central liturgical experience in the life of the Episcopal community. Furthermore, the deacon may not be elected a "deputy" (delegate) to the national Church's triennial General Convention (legislative body) or to membership on an assortment of other governing bodies, such as ecclesiastical courts. A deacon's salary is generally lower than that of a priest, and his or her chances for employment are severely limited, since parishes, chaplaincies, and other church agencies will normally seek priests for employment so that Holy Communion may be celebrated within the agency. The employment liability is especially acute for *women* deacons, since *men* deacons will be ordained priests very soon, and the prospective employer knows this.

Most often the *man* deacon, while limited in function for a short while, is for all practical purposes a "rookie" priest. He knows that, for the good of the Church, he will be ordained soon to the priesthood, the full sacramental ministry of the Church, while the *woman* deacon is left waiting, often unemployed—for months, years—and is told that her situation, too, is "for the good of the Church."

The current Episcopal dilemma has been generated by these conditions. The problem is *not* that women deacons are in any ways deficient or "unworthy." The problem is *not* that there is any canon law forbidding the ordination of women priests (which there is *not*, unlike in Roman Catholic canons).

The problem is that, since the 1970 General Convention officially agreed to affirm the ordination of women as deacons purportedly on "the same basis as men" (!), some several scores of women have been accepted, educated, and examined for ordination to the *priesthood*; have passed all tests with flying colors (usually with outstanding scores, recommendations, and credentials); and have been ordained deacons, with the expectation that the priesthood is "right around the corner."

We have found ourselves *waiting* for somebody—some future General Convention perhaps, some bold bishop perhaps—to confirm *now* what our parishes and dioceses agree to be our call to the priesthood of the church—*now*.

In the late fall of 1973, a woman deacon said to her bishop as she urged him to proceed with her ordination to the priesthood:

"Oh, I could wait until the General Convention gives me permission to be who I am. I could wait, and I might. But, Bishop, when this permission is someday given and you ordain me to the priesthood, you'll be ordaining only a shell. Because by then, through these years of disobedience to God on my part, I will have lost my soul."

From the outset, I have appreciated the bishop of New York, Paul Moore, Jr.'s, *humanness*. He is not a pretentious person.

Paul Moore was affirmative of my call to the priesthood. By the fall of 1972, I had been accepted as a postulant and candidate for ordination to the priesthood. The bishop and I shared not only a hope, but naively an assumption, that the 1973 General Convention would clarify and make explicit the canonical possibility for the ordination of women to the priesthood. Thus began my active involvement with other women and men throughout the Church who were working hard for a reinterpretation of ordination canons. More significant than any specific political tasks we undertook was the community that was seeded among us and began to grow. Women deacons; women candidates, postulants, and aspirants; laywomen; laymen; clergymen found each other and nurtured bonds among ourselves on the basis of not only our common goal, but moreover, our common vision of what the Church is called to be.

Since I was to be ordained a deacon in the summer of 1973, I spent the better part of the preceding year learning something of what it means to be a deacon, a servant, immersing myself in the needs of New York City. Alongside several academic requirements for graduation from seminary and for ordination, I worked part-time both as a therapist in a residency program for homeless adolescent boys and as a student-chaplain at Bellevue Hospital. In the seminary itself, I participated in a "core" group, an experimental, voluntary grouping of students who had contracted to shape and implement our own education, employing whatever resources we needed, individually and as a group. I continued in therapy and in consciousness-raising. The support that I received that year from student peers, supervisors, and people to whom I ministered was instructive.

If there is an order of ministry which has incorporated historically the call to do what is just, it is the diaconate. One of the charges made to a deacon upon ordination is that she, or he, "interpret to the Church the needs, concerns, and hopes of the world."[8]

Upon my ordination to the diaconate, I would "solemnly engage to conform to the doctrine, discipline, and worship" of the Church. This was one part of an oath[9] that I certainly believed would support my attempts to interpret to the Church the needs, concerns, and hopes of the world. I had struggled with this "Oath of Conformity" prior to my ordination as a deacon, knowing that I could not commit myself unconditionally to conform to any set of unjust, hence ungodly, expectations. After conversation, study, and prayer, I had come to realize that the essence of that oath is in its expectation that any person who takes it will attempt to conform herself to the movement of the Holy Spirit. The Bible and the tradition should keep purposeful check on a person's simply "doing her own thing." One's conscience and common sense should keep check on the manipulation of either Bible or tradition (including canon law) for ungodly purposes. I had come to realize that neither doctrine nor discipline nor worship, nor even the Holy Scriptures themselves, would offer easy answers or clear channels of accountability—"cheap grace" —to the deacon, priest, or bishop of the Church. After ordination, I would be faced with the same ambiguities, complexities, decisions, and risks that I had always faced.

By the time I was ordained a deacon, June 9, 1973, I was aware that central to my vocation would be a ministry of reformation within the Church, for the sake of the world; within the world, for the sake of the Church; and within myself, for the sake of my soul, which is the God-in-me, as in all. *Ongoing reformation.*

In late August, 1973, my sister deacon from New York, Carol Anderson and I went camping in Nova Scotia. We had looked forward to getting away from New York and our respective routines prior to the Louisville Convention. We needed refreshment. Furthermore, we wanted this time together, for in the course of our relationship, Carol and I had discovered something important about ourselves: While she leans toward prudence and I toward adventure, Carol and I are of a common theological mind. Our perceptions of world, self, and God are often identical. We had taken note frequently, with appreciation, of the checks and balances we brought to each other. We needed to be together to discuss our shared concerns about the Episcopal Church and our participation in it. We also needed to put our heads together about our alternatives should the General Convention again vote down women's ordination.

Relaxing in Putney, Vermont, the weekend prior to Philadelphia ordination, July, 1974.

We spent the better part of our week patching a hole in the tent, listening to bagpipes, combing beaches, collecting lobster crates and driftwood, reading, and discussing things that mattered to us. We agreed that a negative vote in convention would have to be challenged—perhaps by future votes, certainly by action. We agreed that a positive vote in convention might mean very little in the accomplishment of basic change in structures and theology of the church. We agreed that the Church must change *radically*—at its roots—if it were to be a viable institution for people in search of soul, people called to a corporate mission of healing brokenness, building community, and facilitating justice—essentially one and the same mission.

The two of us vented anger about the arrogance of a number of Episcopalians who speak of the "One Holy Catholic Apostolic Church" as if such an entity has a magical monopoly on Jesus Christ. We recognized the *fear* in which such theological and ecclesiastical arrogance is rooted—fear of all that lurks without, fear of "the other," fear of the unknown, fear of each other, fear especially among the clergy who have created and perpetuated the delusion that the Body of Christ can best be adored within sanctuary walls and the tomes of tradition.

Given this fairly pervasive clerical fear, acted out often as a fear of women, could there be any wonder that sooner or later an Episcopal male cleric would hit, or otherwise physically assault, an Episcopal female cleric?

My surprise at being scratched on the hand and cursed by a young male priest as I held the chalice from which he had sipped was less great than my surprise at many people's inability to believe that such a thing could happen. Recently I was told that a young priest and outspoken opponent of women's ordination has boasted to a Canadian churchwoman that he himself is the man who scratched me. Interestingly enough, I know this boyish "defender of the faith" and he is not the one. Wishful thinking perhaps. If looks could kill, we'd all be dead.

> *In case you're getting any hate-mail, please consider this a piece of love-mail.*
>
> —Letter to me from priest,
> Diocese of New York, winter, 1975.

Over a period of several years, I had a number of sequential dreams. In each there hung on the wall a picture of a man in a loincloth. The man was holding a lamb. In one of the last of these dreams, in the summer of 1973, shortly before General Convention, I dreamt that I was puttering about my dormitory room in New York's Union Theological Seminary. To my surprise, I saw a picture hanging on the wall. It was of a young woman in a loincloth. She was holding a lamb. I moved closer to the picture and noticed that the lamb was wriggling, and the woman moving with it in her hold, so as not to drop it or let it go. I edged still closer and watched the lamb grow larger, and larger, and larger, until I could see nothing in the frame except a lamb who was coming to life and moving from the picture towards me. I heard the woman, by then invisible, say to me, *"Take her, she's yours!"* And the lamb plopped into my arms.

The dream continued: I was walking up Broadway with the lamb in my arms. I did not know what to do with it. The lamb was heavy. It was "baa-a-aing" and nuzzling me as if it were hungry. I had a feeling that if I were to put it down long enough to search for something it could eat, it would get hit by traffic or be terrified and run away. Yet I could not carry it much further. It was too heavy. I began crying. I came into a long, seemingly endless, row of rooms. In each room sat some person, significant in my life, and to each person I offered the lamb. Each person refused to take it. Each looked at me—some tenderly, some angrily—and said to me, *"Take her, she's yours!"* I awoke from this dream, sobbing. I felt as if the lamb were actually lying across my breasts pinning me down by its very being.

I found it still painful—and frightening—to claim myself, my own authority, stand up, and walk on my own.

In September, 1973, Carol and I, along with dozens of women deacons and seminarians, headed for Louisville, Kentucky, for the General Convention of the Episcopal Church. With our notebooks filled with lists of deputies and indications of how each might vote and our knowledge of at least one person in most dioceses to whom we might turn for information, we were equipped as politicians. We knew already that the vote would be close, and that if we were to lose, it would be only barely by a voting system in which divided bloc votes (2–2 splits among the 4 votes to which each lay and clerical deputation is entitled) are registered, effectually, as "no." Hence, even with a majority vote (as much as 75%), an issue can—and often does—lose.

We realized also that our efforts to win must be tidy and attractive. We must smile, be friendly, dress fashionably enough to be "ladies" and appropriately enough to be "clergy." Like Miss America contestants, we must be on our best behavior.

Unlike Miss America contestants, we had few role models. We must be careful, lest we be so real—so human, happy, angry, enthusiastic, honest, tearful—as to offend those who were looking for some excuse to reject us.

This game-playing got to me. I began to feel plastic, shiny, mechanical, and I began to view others the same way. Every day brought with it increased estrangement from myself. Passing empty pleasantries with members of the Committee for the Apostolic Ministry (an opponent group) was an exercise in nonsense. Shying away from other controversial interest groups, so as not to risk tarnishing our image, was an exercise in hypocrisy. Listening silently to a prospective voter who believed there is too much "black power" in the church was my participation in racial discrimination.

Something was wrong. Surely I could be open to those who disagreed with me. But I could be so, I realized, only if I were to allow myself the freedom to argue earnestly with them, vigorously reject their views, all the while wearing the kind of hair, clothes, and buttons I wanted to. I had never been comfortable flirting, conniving, or using cunning to win dates, offices, or honors. I could not do so to win ordination.

At the convention, we received word of Jennie Moore's death. Mrs. Moore, a writer, community leader, and Bishop Paul Moore's wife, had been dying of cancer for months. Her death was no surprise to any of us, but it hit me like a ton of bricks. I had not known, or met, Jennie Moore, but I had known Paul and a number of Jennie's friends. I was aware not only of Paul's grief, but also of the hard blow her terminal illness had dealt those in her life who knew her to be a strong woman who was continuing to discover new things about herself. Oddly, I felt as if in Jennie Moore's death something within me had been symbolically shattered. Perhaps it was the nondurable plasticity of the conventional game we were playing.

When we learned of her death, the women deacons from New York bounded out of our political roles into the composition of a message which we wired to Paul. We found our hearts engaged in something real and human..

On the following day, October 4, some forty women deacons (none of whom could be deputies, since deacons are officially disenfranchised) listened to clerical and lay deputies give reasons why women cannot, or may not, be ordained priests:[10]

—Jesus Christ, who was and is the Great High Priest, was a man. The ordained priest is Christ's icon (i.e., Christ's image). The ordained priest is an *alter Christus*, "another Christ." The maleness of Christ was no accident and is today still no accident as the priest, the icon of Christ, stands before the people who are the Church, His Bride, and sacrifices His life for her in the breaking of His Body (the bread) and the shedding of His Blood (the wine). It is no more possible for a woman to be ordained a priest than for a jackass to be ordained a priest.

—The twelve apostles were men. If Jesus had wanted women to be priests, he would have chosen a woman disciple. In order to be faithful to the apostolic succession, as we are an heir to it, we must be faithful to its maleness.

—Women can be, and are, deacons, of course. They should work hard to build a stronger diaconate for the good of the Church.

—We will damage our relationship to the Roman Catholic and Orthodox communions if we ordain women priests. We should wait, at the very least, until we have a consensus among the entire Anglican Communion (Church of England and other Anglican bodies).

—There is already an oversupply of clergy in the Church. We really don't have room for women priests.

—Woman's place is in the home. This change would weaken the fabric of the family. It would heighten sexual confusion and lead, eventually, to divorce, abortion, homosexuality, and other "ills."

—Women are simply unfit to be priests. They cry too easily. They can't go out alone at night. They are needed in the nursery and in the kitchen, places where their maternal instincts and feelings can best be employed. After all, that's the way God made them!

—Just look at those women deacons! Aggressive, dressed in pants, acting like a bunch of men. If we have to have women priests, let's wait until we can have some *real women*.

An exercise in imagination for my male reader:[11] My brother, imagine, just imagine for a minute, that at age 27, you are ordained a deacon in the Church; and that three months later, the General Convention of the church (90 percent of its deputies female) discusses in your presence whether or not men should be allowed to be priests. Neither you nor any deacon is allowed a voice or vote. Church policy. You listen to the reasons given by those who believe that you should *not* be allowed to be a priest:

—Since there is only one Great High Priest—Jesus Himself—according to the book of Hebrews, we need not fear that "maleness" be left out of the fullness of the ordained ministry. Jesus Christ, in His spiritual presence, provides enough of the masculine for all time and all people. What is indispensable to the priesthood of the Church is the *feminine* component: faith, intuitive receptivity from God in order to serve as a vehicle by which others can come to faith. Men are incapable of serving in this way. Alas, it is no more possible for a man to be ordained a priest than for a jackass to be ordained a priest.

—The witnesses to the Resurrection were women. If God had wanted men to be priests, She'd have sent them to the empty tomb.

—Indeed, men can be deacons, since the diaconate is best modeled after Jesus's twelve male disciples. Men should be encouraged to be deacons, since the church needs a stronger diaconate.

—Even if men *should* be allowed such ordination, we cannot jeopardize our relationship to Rome or to the rest of the Anglican Communion. We must wait until the Holy Catholic Church agrees with us before taking this important step.

—There are too many women priests as it is! We do not have room for men priests. It would be unfair to them.

—Having men as priests would produce sexual confusion in the church and society. Can you imagine seeing men in long skirts! And expecting men to play women's roles like listening, comforting, and preparing and serving food to others. This would destroy the family as we know it and lead to "perversion."

—Men are simply unfit emotionally and physically for the work of a priest. Their presence is needed elsewhere—as carpenters, plumbers, occupations that require machismo, muscles, and brawn. After all, that's the way God made them!

—Just look at those men deacons! Running around in bright-colored clothes and praying like a bunch of women! If we must have men priests, let's wait until we can have some *real men*.

Quietly we watched women's ordination go down to defeat.
I saw my sister deacon Carol's lip quivering. I noticed that my sister seminarian Huntley's lovely face was contorted. Across the stadium, I caught a glimpse of the woman who had become known to many of us as "the bishop to the women," deacon Sue Hiatt. Her head was bowed. I felt nauseated, sick, and immobile, as my eyes gazed out upon the arena of deputies who had torn us apart as surely as if they had been lions and we, those early Christians whom no one would believe.
Suddenly a deputy from Pennsylvania, Mr. Donald Belcher, sprang to his feet on the convention floor and took the microphone nearest him. He cried out:

Mr. President, Members of the House:
I rise to a point of personal privilege. There is a priest in the Diocese of Pennsylvania who has counseled many of us lovingly and wisely on the subject of the ordination of women. Anticipating the possible defeat of this resolution, two nights ago I sat alone and wondered what I could possibly say to that loving and wise priest to whom the ordination of women meant so much. And I decided I would say:

Thank you for your gifts so far;
Thank you for your courage which I do not have;
Thank you for the hope you will, God willing, continue to
clasp close to you and radiate to us.
   And do not despair, Susan Hiatt, for in God's eyes you are priest
indeed. They cannot close you in; they cannot defeat you, for in
Christ you are free.

> O Mary, don't you weep, don't you mourn.
> O Mary, don't you weep, don't you mourn.
> Pharaoh's army got drownded.
> O Mary, don't you weep.
> —Negro Spiritual

I will not forget Sue Hiatt's stoic silence, Union Seminary
President Bishop Brooke Mosley's restrained tears, and the
Bishop of Pennsylvania Robert DeWitt's eyes cast downward in
thoughtful intensity. I will not forget the drifting together of
many as if to a wake, much in the manner of elephants who
press close together to mourn when one in their midst has died.

The day was upon me when I would begin to admit that I
could no longer bow down to the golden calf, the phallic idol of
Christendom. I would begin to see that "women's ordination" is
not a matter which belongs to the arena of a general convention.
*A vote is to be taken when one is faced with viable alternatives,
such as old and new prayer books. Whereas prayer book revision
is a matter of taste, women's ordination is a matter of justice.*
And as in all matters of justice, one is faced with a choice
essentially between the worship of God and the worship of an
idol—in this case the phallus of male anatomy, every bit as
much an idol as the breasts of fertility goddesses might be considered. By no stretch of imagination is phallic idolatry, the
adoration of male genitalia, a viable alternative for a community
of the Christian faithful. In Louisville, it occurred to me that, on
this issue, we have no business attempting to win favor with man

and votes from him. People seldom vote for justice until it is too late.

> And he [Moses] took the calf which they had made, and burnt it with fire, and ground it to powder, and scattered it upon the water, and made the people of Israel drink it.
>
> Exodus 32:20

A number of us gathered in a motel suite and considered our alternatives. Most of us had no question that there should be an ordination of women priests in the near future. We had many questions about how, who, when, where, and which bishops, priests, women deacons, and laypeople among those present might choose to participate in the ordaining community.

We left Louisville to return to our respective communities. When I returned to Union Seminary and to St. Mary's parish (West Harlem, New York City, not to be confused with St. Mary the Virgin near Times Square, where women priests are considered anathema), I was met by an extension of the same mourning-community I had left in Louisville. Women and men, Episcopalians and others, had received the news from Kentucky as one would receive news of a friend's death.

Students and faculty at Union had gathered in vigil while we were gone and had written and compiled reflections which they shared with us on our return. They were tokens of an assurance we had never doubted; among them:

Sisters:

You *have* the ministry which is in Christ Jesus—in you as well! *You have it.* It is yours by the power of the Spirit, speaking in your spirits. None can take it from you, for we who have been ministered to by you have confirmed it already through the healing your presence has brought to us. Whatever happens at Louisville is beside the point with respect to this, your ministry. It is not beside the point with respect to what the Church can do and be in our time, however. The decision being made in Louisville is whether the Church will choose what is life-giving, or whether it will continue to walk in fear, apostasy, death.

My prayer for you is that you stand in your calling, bearing in power the struggle between grace and demonry going on there in Louisville.

My prayer is also one of gratitude for myself, that whatever happens, you will soon be here again.

My prayer for the Church is that it may be delivered from the demons, to discern the Spirit in the spirits. It needs that deliverance. There is much it could still do for human beings if that deliverance were given. May those who have eyes discern *what decision* is actually being made.

Why do they think it's so great when they give us "permission" to be whole?

I hope they raise a stink, Lord. Let's get the kingdom all the nearer.

Why am I fortunate enough to be a member of a denomination, by birth, that already grants women the ministry? Or, perhaps, my Episcopal sisters, as other women in history, will experience more of God's message by having stood up for that in which they believe revealed in His word.

Grant that all brothers and sisters share a commitment together for the good of all. For, after all, we are all captives as long as there are those oppressed.

Dear God:
How about a little Old Testament vindication!!

> The strength, the pounding strength
> The power, the forging power
> The truth, the sounding truth
> The hands, the joining hands
> Pound Strength, Forge Power
> Sound Truth, Join Hands.
> We will stand in strength,
> Power, truth, and unity.
> We will not be broken.
> We will become.

The struggle, the pain, the defeat, the hope, the determination could not be confined to, or contained within, a small group of Episcopal women deacons and seminarians. Ours was a Church issue, a men's issue, a lay issue, an ecumenical issue, a human issue broad-based in its connection to all issues of institutional justice.

Distress was apparent among the people of St. Mary's parish. Both Emily Hewitt and I had spent time as deacons at St. Mary's. The parishioners were hopeful that the bishop of New York would rally the Standing Committee of the Diocese and move ahead with the ordination of New York's six women deacons to the priesthood. In early November, 1973, we six met with Paul Moore and asked him to think about ordaining us. He told us he would consider it, but that his initial reaction was negative.

Several weeks later, five bishops (Moore of New York, Spears of Rochester, DeWitt of Pennsylvania, Ogilby also of Pennsylvania, Mead of Delaware) met with nine women deacons (the six from New York: Carol Anderson, Julia Sibley, Emily Hewitt, Marie Moorefield, Barbara Schlachter, me; plus Sue Hiatt, Merrill Bittner, and Betty Schiess). Together with Harvey Guthrie from the Episcopal Theological School and Tom Pike from New York's Calvary Church, the group spent the better part of twenty-four hours hashing and rehashing the pros and cons of an "irregular" ordination. The women deacons felt strongly that we should move full-speed ahead. The bishops were unsure, not of whether we were ready to be priested, but rather of whether such action might prove "counterproductive" or of whether each of them, individually, would choose to make the move at this time.

Twenty-two hours into the discussion, having reached an impasse, we deacons walked out. We could tell that these bishops shared with us the belief that such an ordination would be *morally right*. We had witnessed, it seemed to us, their inability to comprehend the *moral imperative* of the matter, for they seemed unable to comprehend the corporate pain of increasing numbers of churchwomen. We could tell them about our pain. We could show them our pain from time to time. But they were men. They were not women, and we could not give them our pain, pour it into their psyches any more than a black person can give a white person her humiliation from having been spat at when she stopped to sip from the "wrong" water fountain.

> And I don't want to be trite
> but yes, it makes a difference.
> Sister, keep up the fight,
> continue your insistence.[12]

By late fall of 1973, a number of Episcopal women had begun to speak determinatively of action. Behind several of us lay the experience of meeting with bishops who shared our concern but not our urgency. Ahead of us, we would have the occasions of coming together and acting on concern in a spirit of shared urgency.

The urgency became first most publicly apparent on December 15, 1973, at the ordination of five men deacons to the priesthood in the Diocese of New York. Five women deacons from the diocese were presented at this time by Episcopal laypeople and clergy (in several cases, our own rectors and vestries) for ordination as priests. The sixth woman deacon, Marie Moorefield, was sick and could not fly in from her Kansas home, although she had the endorsement of her New York rector and vestry.

The women deacons had met at length to consider in what way we might bring our case before the bishop and other people in the diocese. At first, we thought only of a "witness" to our dilemma: we would be presented for ordination, we would be refused, and our rejection would be a public symbol of the injustice being perpetrated by the Church on its own. We felt that Episcopal and general public needed to be made aware of what was taking place within an institution that calls itself the Body of Christ.

We had not decided whether to talk to Paul Moore about our plans, for we had not concluded whether his awareness, and hence, his approval or his admonition, would impede or assist us in what we were trying to do.

Paul Moore found out about our plans for the witness. Several days before the ordination, he, Carol Anderson, John Coburn (Carol's rector and employer), and I met to discuss it.

Carol and I stated, yet again, why "the issue"—i.e., the immediacy of our lives and vocations—seemed so important to us. Paul Moore and John Coburn dealt with us sympathetically, and yet in apparent annoyance that we believed they could do more than they were doing to "further the cause."

"You could *ordain* us, Paul," I suggested seriously.

John Coburn stated emphatically that this was not so.

"Of course he could!" I insisted "We're ready to be ordained priests. We'll be presented and taking the vows. Paul could lay his hands on our heads and ordain us. He *could*, but he *won't*."

The two men continued to look at me as if they were thoroughly puzzled.

Carol and I continued to speak of justice, human rights, and being female in a Church in which male members are the ones with the power to say yes or no to such possibilities as the one we presented. And the two male priests—both bright, sensitive, earnest clergymen with longstanding commitments to justice and human rights—stared at us as if we were speaking a foreign language.

Not until Carol began to explicate our conversation about "justice" in such a way as to assure the rector and the bishop that we were indeed talking about "God," did their faces register any signs of comprehension. It felt as if our experiences—our feelings, our goals, our vocations, our perceptions and concerns —lacked viability, credibility, and import unless we were to articulate them in the language of the Book of Common Prayer and to justify them by the canonical structures of a tradition that, from the beginning, has taken no account of women's experiences or our yearnings for a freedom to be who we are.

This makes me think of my college friend May's trying to convince me that the war in Vietnam was not only wrong, but also worthy of our active protests. She might as well have been speaking Vietnamese to me. It was not that I did not *care*; it was that I did not care *enough*. And, in 1965, I still had "faith" in the United States Government to see things through with righteousness.

Perhaps New York's women deacons lacked "faith" in ecclesiastical structures to see things through with righteousness. On the evening preceding the ordination of men, the five of us women met, along with spouses and others who would be with us the next day. We decided that, during the service, one of us would rise in objection to the exclusion of women deacons from the ordination. She would speak for the rest of us, asking that the ordination not take place without us. We would then take the vows, and hopefully, be ordained! As if suddenly, somewhat unconsciously and certainly unwittingly, we were not intending to make simply a *witness*. We were intending to be ordained to the priesthood. True to catholic theology, the symbol would be real.

We were unable to conclude what we would do should Paul Moore refuse to ordain us, as he had indicated would be the case. We were hoping against hope: an exercise in pain, but an experience in imagination that would carry us far beyond that day. Several of us felt that, if we were rejected, we should plant ourselves kneeling in the sanctuary, an offensive symbol of an offensive injustice. Others of us believed that we should instead leave the cathedral, a symbol of the brokenness of the Body. We could agree only that the five of us would make a corporate response and that we could not know what it was to be until the moment bore down upon us.

At the next morning's ordination, in the Cathedral of St. John the Divine, the Bishop of New York asked, as required, for knowledge of "any impediment or crime because of which we should not proceed." Speaking for the others from a draft prepared by all of us, I moved to the lectern:

My sisters and brothers, there is an impediment because of which we should not proceed.

There are ten deacons here today. All ten of us have been presented, but only five of us are listed in the order of service. Each of us has been called by God to the priesthood of the Church, examined by bishops and others, and found qualified, and ready, to be ordained priests.

Yet five of us have been told by the Episcopal Church that we cannot be ordained today, because—and only because—we are women.

Ordination is a sacrament, an outward and visible sign of an inward and spiritual grace. The grace of God. A unifying grace that makes us one in the Body of Jesus Christ. A grace that destroys all barriers to unity, including the barrier of gender. And yet our gender—our womanhood—has been interpreted by the Church as the specific barrier to our partaking in this holy sacrament of ordination.

If the service proceeds without us, the sacrament of ordination will be used to perpetrate injustice. It will be an outward and visible sign of the intentional sin and division of the Church. The sacrament will be debased just as much as it would be if black people were excluded.

To sin is human, a condition in which all of us participate. To perpetuate willfully this sin—this intentional brokenness, this prolonged injustice, this exclusion of women throughout history—is a condition we find intolerable. Especially as the Church perpetuates it in the name of God.

If this ordination does proceed without the women deacons, let those here know what is being said to all of us by the Church:

that the structural unity of the Protestant Episcopal Church is more important than the unity of the people of God;

that peace in the House of Bishops is more important than justice; that the law of man, established by church convention, is more compelling than the Gospel of the Lord.

We know, of course, what a special day this is for our brothers, these five male deacons, who are here to be ordained to the priesthood. We did not come to block you, but to join you.

We are also aware of the uncomfortable position in which our pastor and friend, Bishop Paul Moore, finds himself. There are precedents in Church history for this uncomfortable position. Jesus himself was no stranger to the snares of Pharisaic law. Paul, we cannot spare you the discomfort of your position.

We are asking to be included in this service not only for our sake, but for the sake of other women; for the sake of all women and men; for the sake of the Episcopal Church. We intend to be examined and to take the vows that follow in the service.

We are asking you, Paul, as Bishop of New York—together with other bishops present—to ordain us today, along with our brothers.

> Statement signed by Carol Anderson,
> Emily Hewitt, Carter Heyward,
> Barbara Schlachter, Julia Sibley.

December 15, 1973

As we expected and did not expect, the bishop turned us down. Paul Moore's expression, as I looked up at him from my kneeling position, was one of anguish. He meant us no harm, no injustice, no "personal" rejection. Yet, as a bishop of the Church, he had dealt us as real a blow as if he had flailed us with his crozier. We meant him no harm, and yet our very beings, bursting free, would continue to batter him. Members of families set at odds, as if at war, against each other.

Like our brother deacons, we had been educated, examined, and supported by our parishes and the diocese itself as candidates for ordination to the priesthood. Like the men, we had passed all physical, psychiatric, academic, and spiritual examinations. Like our male colleagues, we had been ordained deacons for at least six months. (Two of us, Carol Anderson and Julia Sibley, had been deacons for two years.)

Surely our bishop had realized, when he encouraged us pastorally and financially in our vocational pursuits, accepted us as

A group of women deacons who are seeking ordination to the priesthood stage a peaceful demonstration at the Cathedral of St. John the Divine as a group of men deacons are ordained to the priesthood. December 15, 1973.

candidates, and gave us the final examinations for priesthood that we would indeed want to be priests; and that the communities in which we worked would expect us to be.

But there we stood, like the child who has been taken swimming and is not permitted to go into the water, or the doctor who has served well an internship and residency, graduated at the top of her class, and is not permitted to practice because she is female.

For several seconds we knelt immobile at Paul Moore's feet. Then, spontaneously, we rose and strode quickly down the center aisle towards the mammoth bronze exit of the cathedral. At least a third of the congregation followed us out. For five minutes, I wept into the shoulder of my clergy presenter and friend, Brooke Mosley, himself a bishop and president of Union Seminary. This was one of few times in my life that I have felt as if my heart were breaking. Each of the five of us, it seemed, had found a space in the back of the cathedral to be alone, or with whomever she could be, to tend her wounds.

Within half an hour, we had gathered among friends at Union Seminary for an agapé meal, in which we could share our experience of the body and blood of Christ. We made our communion with integrity.

The next months incorporated both pain and premonition of what was to come. In April, 1974, St. Mary's church officially requested that Emily and I be ordained priests on May 17, the date which had been scheduled for the ordination to the priesthood of our parish colleague, Dan Jones.

Dear Bishop Moore and Fr. Pike [Chairman of Standing Committee]:

At its meeting on April 16, 1974, the Vestry of St. Mary's Church noted that we have three candidates to the priesthood, all of whom we warmly and equally support as members and pastors of this congregation. They are: the Rev. Emily Hewitt, the Rev. I. Carter Heyward, and the Rev. Daniel B. Jones.

Enclosed are the necessary executed documents for the Revs. Hewitt and Heyward, except for Ms. Hewitt's Application which will come under separate cover. You already have the necessary documents and authorization for the Rev. Jones. We request that these three deacons be together ordained to the priesthood in St. Mary's Church on Friday, May 17, 1974.

Because you may have questions about our request, members of the Vestry are available to meet with you to discuss these questions at your earliest convenience. . . .

> Very truly yours,
> Allen Mellen
> Vestry Clerk

Dear Mr. Mellen:

Your letter from the Vestry of St. Mary's Church was read at yesterday's meeting of the Standing Committee. . . . I think you would be pleased with the thoughtful and concerned discussion that took place around the question of the ordination of women and the appropriateness of any action by the Standing Committee.

The minutes of the Standing Committee will include the statement that "it concurs in the opinion of the Diocesan and Suffragan Bishops of New York that women cannot at this time be ordained to the priesthood." ...

The ordination of women to the priesthood is a painful and complex matter which we shall continue to deal with in the foreseeable future. Let us hope that the need for such correspondence as ours will some day soon be unnecessary.

> Faithfully yours,
>
> Thomas F. Pike
>
> President, Standing Committee

Nearly two weeks after the first, another letter would be mailed to the bishop, this time on behalf of the congregation itself:

Dear Bishop Moore:

I appreciated hearing from Fr. Secor [the rector] of your recent conversations with him regarding our Vestry's support of all three of our deacons for ordination to the priesthood on May 17....

Your comments, Fr. Pike's letter to me, and Fr. Pike's telephone conversation with our past warden ... were reported to the 151st Annual Meeting of St. Mary's held on April 28. Fr. Secor and all three of our deacons were present at that meeting. It is probably important for you and the Standing Committee to know that our clergy are in no way "lobbying" with or pressuring the congregation. As is the Vestry, the clergy are highly aware that for St. Mary's, this is an essentially pastoral/congregational matter about which we are deeply concerned and highly perplexed....

The Congregation of St. Mary's enthusiastically supports all three of our deacons as being fully qualified for the priesthood ... and continues to hope that the Bishops and Standing Committee of our diocese will change their positions so that our three deacons may become priests on May 17, 1974.

The Congregation of St. Mary's ... sincerely desires the personal counsel of the Bishops and Standing Committee and hopes we might have mutual conversations in this regard in the near future.

The Congregation of St. Mary's will undertake a special Christian Education endeavor both within its own parish and with any other similarly concerned parishes so that *the issue of ordaining women who have been called into the priesthood is perceived not simply as a political one or just as a vocational issue for the women so called, but rather as the congregational/pastoral issue of Christ's Church, which we deeply feel it to be.* (Italics mine.)

No matter what the final decisions of the Bishops and Standing Committee regarding the May 17 service of ordination . . . *the Congregation will continue to be vitally concerned with and vigorously pursue the issues involved and most particularly the ordination to the priesthood of I. Carter Heyward and Emily Hewitt, members and pastors of St. Mary's.* (Italics mine.)

Thank you, Bishop, for your continuing concern. We realize your present "bind" and are trying to be supportive of your feelings and judgments, rather than of the legalisms which have trapped us all. . . .

> Very truly yours,
> E. Allen Mellen
> Newly Elected Warden, and Clerk

Diocesan response to the pleas of the vestry and congregation was largely bewilderment and anger. Perhaps recalling the events in the cathedral on December 15, the bishops assumed the "worst" and made it clear that they wanted no "demonstration" at this ordination. The ordaining Suffragan Bishop told Dan, in fact, that he would not ordain him if there were to be any demonstrations by "the women." Dan's own bishop, of another diocese, for whom he was being ordained in New York, wrote Dan that he had heard

that there is a possibility that some of the female deacons will try to use the occasion of your ordination as a demonstration to promote their cause. . . . Therefore, I will withdraw my request to the Bishop of New York to ordain you, if this is going to take place. You can come back to _____, and I will ordain you here. If you can be certain that this demonstration will not take place, go ahead with your ordination there, but I will not embarrass the Bishop of New York in any way.

To my knowledge there had been no talk of "demonstrating." When it had become apparent that Emily and I would not be ordained, Dan invited me to preach at the service.

On May 17, St. Mary's rector, wardens, and vestry distributed a statement to members of the congregation at Dan's ordination. Its conclusion read:

> St. Mary's ... will continue to work and pray for the ordination of all of God's children called to the priesthood. Especially we will work and pray for the ordinations of Carter Heyward and Emily Hewitt at the very earliest time.
> Tonight we rejoice with Dan. We are grateful that persons such as Daniel Jones have been called by God and accepted by His Church. We are dismayed that persons such as Carter Heyward and Emily Hewitt have been called by God but rejected by His Church.
> We ask you to pray for Daniel, to pray for Carter and Emily, to pray for our Bishops, to pray for your parish, and to pray for the Church of God.

> *Has it ever occurred to you that if Christ intended women to be priests, He would have chosen at least one of them to be his apostle? There were no females present at the Last Supper.*
> —Letter to me from layman,
> Diocese of New York, winter, 1975.

Not long after Dan's ordination, I had the last of my lamb dreams to date. I was walking along a riverbank and fell into the river. The current was strong, the undertow fierce. I began struggling to swim and soon realized that my efforts were futile. I knew that my only hope was to give in to the current and let myself wash downstream with it towards its end, and so I did. I floated, dived, bobbed, went under, and came up time and again. After minutes, days, years—perhaps a lifetime—I found myself moving in the manner of a fish gracefully down towards the bottom of the river. When I came to rest, I noticed that I had landed on a bed of oysters, which oddly enough were not sharp or painful but rather seemed to provide a cushioned floor on which I could sleep. After a long nap on the riverbed, I woke up and saw, literally galloping towards me across the oyster shells, the lamb. I was ecstatic as she barrelled into my arms, and when she began nuzzling me, a pearl fell out of her mouth into my hand. I awoke, laughing.

We women priests have laughed our way to Philadelphia, New York, Washington, Rochester, Oberlin, Cambridge, Detroit, Woods Hole, and on, believing God to be most surely our authority, in whom resonates a wise, merciful laughter that cuts through the cosmos, transforming people of dread into people of hope.

In faith, the movement among us is irrepressible. Faith, not our working to win votes. Faith, not our certainty about what may happen next. Faith, not our idealism that things will change if we try hard enough. "The Lord said, 'If you had faith as a grain of mustard seed, you could say to this sycamine tree, 'Be rooted up, and be planted in the sea,' and it would obey you'" (Luke 17:6).

When I find myself wondering whether we eleven will ever make it to the Promised Land, I always know in some deep way that we have made it already. Having made it long ago, we celebrated once more our arrival on July 29, 1974. That is what Philadelphia was all about.

> *You have ministered to me and my sisters in a way that I don't even understand completely. At the Riverside Service, I felt like it was my birthday. I felt redeemed and that Jesus Christ was sacrificed for me in a way that I have never known before.*
> —Letter to me from laywoman,
> Diocese of Ohio, fall, 1974.

In late May, 1974, along with several of my Union Seminary colleagues, I took off for the Esalen Institute in Big Sur, California.

Esalen was no heaven. It was simply a time and a space for solitude and prayer; for relationship and new experiences. In the middle of the month a phone call would come, confirming what we had been hoping for months: several bishops were willing to ordain women deacons to the priesthood if we wanted to take the step at this time. Esalen was an offering to me of resources by which I would make spiritual retreat in preparation for experiences I had barely dared to dream.

From my journal, June 2, 1974: It seems as if I've died and gone to heaven. Spellbound by the vast aqua space sparkling with red and gold emanations from the brilliant sun, set on the sea's horizon like a steady beach ball, I sit like a crystal, reflecting the silence and color that surrounds me. The bus swerves in smooth strokes around coastal mountain curves, south from Monterey along the legendary Pacific stretch which reaches toward Big Sur, where I will spend the month with other ministers at Esalen. We are guests of Jean and Sidney Lanier—she, a Gestalt therapist; he, an Episcopal priest; both, spiritual questers and, for the moment, a catalyst around which fourteen of us have been invited to explore various dimensions of religious experience.

June 3: Feelings: calm, quiet, alone. Womanly, childlike, expectant, reserved, warm, somewhat anxious. Powerful. Prayerful. Sewn together as a patchwork quilt with its own peculiar pattern, I feel less ripped into pieces now than I have for a long while.

If God comes to us as a body, does this not give us some clue that, if we are to be aware of God, we must be aware of our bodies? It seems to me that a Christian, of all people, should know the significance of the body! I have been so seldom in touch with my own. As if "it" were a shell, simply an encasement of "me," and as if I can ignore "it" and get on with "being myself" in ignorance of "it": my body, myself, me. "Fat" is not simply a yellow organic paste that lines the skin; it is related to, produced out of, all that I am. If my body feels heavy to me, it is because I am weighted down.

June 4: The Church feels weighty to me. I feel discouraged. I am enraged!

June 6: I must build some internal bridges between now and later, between Esalen and New York. Church problems will not be resolved here at Esalen. But being here among other ministers, including five Episcopalians, is helpful in terms of reality testing. I am not alone in my observations, my feelings, my concerns.

June 7: Thank God for [Bishop] Bob DeWitt! He's one of few men in my life, especially my Church life, who seems not to *fear* me or to take offense at my struggling for a rightful place to be and grow within the Church. One of the few to whom I do not have to be forever "explaining myself" or attempting to justify my feelings. One of few "authority figures" before whom I am not expected to bow and scrape ("Yes, sir; Of course, sir; Indeed, sir; I will, sir") in order to "show respect." He is not afraid of losing his authority, for he seems to know that the real authority on which he lives and works cannot be lost. I detect moving through him the authority of the Holy Spirit.

June 8: This brings me to the question of "authority," certainly the central issue in my life and, I believe, the life of the Church. *In raising the issue of "women's ordination," we must be careful always to raise the issue of authority which rests at the heart of the matter.*

The only real problem I have is that of authority, within which all other problems spring into being and find their rest. What is my authority? What is my God? From what, or whom, do I take my signals? On what basis do I decide, act, evaluate, live? Big questions, and not too big to answer. Not to answer them is not to be at all. The only one who can answer for me is me. There is no person, no book, no tradition, no Church, no story that is my authority, unless I know it as my own. Unless it is mine.

I need space in which to be alone. I believe I am learning something about prayer. I need to claim occasions daily for myself in which I can quietly allow myself the awareness of the Holy Spirit's movement making organic, mystical connection to all creation.

June 9: What is at stake is my soul. What is affected is my vocation—broadly construed, my life. The question of authority touches all that I am and do.

June 11: A vision: There was a fire in that fireplace. I was afraid. I remember inviting "fear" into myself in order to name it, and in the tradition of the casting out of demons, to expel it. It's as though I were staring into the face of evil. Through the flames came the faces of many people, not evil people, but people like myself to whom I have given up my authority; people to whom I have given responsibility for *my* decisions, *my* feelings, *my* actions; people at whom I have later been angry for "trying to run my life."

June 12: What do you do when, expecting to see a Queen, you look in the mirror and see a Jester?

I had to laugh.

The time has come to start withdrawing my projections. To own up to the authority I have given others over my life. To admit that I have given the Church a power to define me, and to devastate me. To realize that some part of my anger is not at "the Church"—its bishops or others—but rather at myself for putting such stock in others' opinions of me, descriptions of me, and decisions about my life which I can choose to accept or reject on the basis of what I know about myself.

June 13: And he said to them, "Come away by yourselves to a lonely place, and rest awhile" (Mark 6:31).

To sisters, brothers, strangers, self:

Somewhere and sometime I knew you.
I knew you well.
I knew you distantly and deeply.
You and I were different
Beings, Bodies
All in one.
Your eyes were my eyes.
You saw what I saw.
Your way was my way.
Wisdom was our way.

We went separate ways, all of us.
The androgyne cracked, dividing itself
Male and Female
Created it them.
Person and person, created it them.
Plant and plant, rock and rock, dog and dog, created it them
Alien and bonded
Separate and connected
Alone, and together alone
All of us went journeying towards reunion.

Towards a unity not to be kept, nor forewarned, nor avoided
      Not to be welcomed, nor gained cheaply
    A unity predicated by its own acceptance, in whole and in part,
      Prior to its coming
    A unity unknown: accepted in faith, vision, madness, and rage.
    An unwelcomed Stranger.

I am scared of such strange unity.
I am scared of looking into your eyes again.
I am scared of seeing myself in yourself.
I prefer to distance these selves from me and call them "you."

I am afraid of you.
I knew it the moment I looked at you
You! Man! Nigger! WASP! Bishop! Bigot! Starving baby! Messed
            up Lover! Teacher! Student! Best friend! You!

  I have escaped before.
  Trembling away from you,

I have escaped myself
and known neither the divine nor the demonic
As holy.

Yes! Somewhere and sometime I have known you
You in particular
You in general.

The temptation has been to give myself to you
To turn myself over to you, into you
To be overpowered, empowered, underpowered
By your strong soul.

Hold me! help me! protect me! defend me!
Forgive me! love me! be me!
And—if it please you—kill me!

It is a time to rest
It is a silent time
Wisdom is not as simple in words
As in the silent vision:

We do not leap without risking.
We do not see without leaping.
We do not know without seeing.
And we are unwise if we do not know
That we are afraid to leap

Then leaping, we tremble towards integrity.

In which the "I" and the "you" become "Thou"
One in being
Embracing the two
And the two billion
And all that has been
And all that will be.

I lay naked on the beach
Sun streaming pouring into me
And me into the sand
An old woman
Wrinkled skin and gray hair
Broken, whole Body.

The bodies of my parents lay in graves behind me.
I lay calm and was pleased to have lived such a life.

I ran to waves and dived in
Going under, coming out
And meeting myself twice over, returned to my sand space:
Old woman, little girl, me now.
The three of us lay down together—
Crying and laughing
Regretful, at peace
Ashamed and proud
Guilty. Absolved.

   Knowing, thinking, nothing
   I knew and saw everything in a flash of faces
   Streaming before me
   Through me, beyond me,
   Carrying me, leaving me
   Alone.

I caught then a glimpse of the Unity:
      an affirmation of what is happening;
    the power of wisdom, and the powerlessness of power.

And I knew that my own growth is yours,
And that to struggle for your being is to enhance my own.
I knew that as long as anyone is a slave, no one is free,
And that no one and nothing is unaffected by what is happening
Here and Now.

I knew

That you are you
Whom I do not know
Whom I do know from somewhere and sometime
And that I am I (old woman, child, fool, wise person, enigmatic
              being, teacher, priest, and more)
Whom I know, of course,
And whom I do not know at all.

I knew

Both of us, and all of us,
As one

Together and alone
Embodied in mysterious process
Of all that we can tentatively name
as either "demonic" or "divine"
Participants in the Journey
Which is tedious growth
Which is Terribly Good
Which is God.

And so, we go.
Your way.
My way.
Meeting
Meeting not.

Sometime and somewhere we will see again
And we will know again

Our way
Wise way
and with Wisdom
We will cry aloud in the street
We will raise our voices
and our tears and our laughter will be one.

We will have learned to dance
And we *will* dance!
There will be no more to say.
Only movement
And music
And at the end of the dance
The silence that has been here all along.

June 14: The trouble with some Episcopalians is that they want to be nursed by the Church forever. They are resistant to weaning. It is tempting. And I myself have fallen into this temptation from time to time, although I have been adamant in my insistence that I have not. The irresponsibility implicit in remaining an adult-infant tied symbiotically to any institutional authority (Church, seminary, Esalen, whatever) for one's life-sustenance is appalling.

I have attempted to stand on my own two feet, as it were, *and* to reap ecclesiastical approval. Can't have it both ways.

So many in the same bag. I listen to Vic, Susan, Jean, Lee, Dallas. The primal screaming, the historic tears: "LET US BE!" But it doesn't work that way. We expend so much energy "asking permission" to feel what we feel, think what we think, do what we need to do, be who we are. And when "they" say "no," we begin making demands.

A movement is in process—from "May I please be who I am?" to "Dammit, let me be who I am!" to "I am who I am." And that, said she, is that.

June 15: I feel taller, healthier, more honest.

June 16: A surprise phone call from a sister deacon asking me to come to a meeting to plan our ordination to the priesthood! "They're really going to do it? I'll believe it when I feel the hands on my head! Of course I'll be there! Yes—I'm ready. Hallelujah!"

June 21: Hands—a symbol of my vocation. Hands write, mold, build, touch, hold, feel, pull, press, push, smooth over, soothe, bless, heal, hit, hurt, break, shield, reach, stretch, embrace, clasp, grasp, make love, celebrate, commune, carry me on.

June 22: I am a person: minister, deacon, student, priest, teacher, prophet, writer, fool and clown, and wise old woman. Little girl as well. Age twenty-eight. I believe in a God of authority, mystery, love, justice, human freedom, anger, compassion, and many surprises. I am fluid and grounded—in sin and grace, in courage and fear. My eyes tell my story—full of sadness and joy, rage and peace, inextricably bound up together.

I am a woman seeking, with my sisters, and some brothers, a priesthood that will be more than a male trophy, a priesthood that could, and will, be born out of nothing less than reformation.

Knowing my own humanness, I am all the more unwilling to join in, or facilitate, my brothers' and sisters' disclaimers of responsibility for what they do—to themselves, to each other, to me. I cannot accept Church tradition, canon law, collegiality among bishops, polls, priority of other issues, timing, misogyny or fear as excuses....

I am unwilling to participate in a game of plastic smiles, new committees, old study projects; a game of watching and waiting as my sisters and I suffocate in coerced compliance;... a game called "Church."

If you, my Episcopal colleagues, have something to say to me, say it! I learn nothing more from your quotes of canon law and scores of faceless saints and bishops sacrosanctly upheld as defenders of some "Holy Catholic Apostolic Church," said to be one and built on the splintered bodies of its outcasts. You always speak the words of someone or thing other than yourself. Always some crutch ("church" misspelled?) to hold you up. I wait for you to stand on your own feet and speak for yourself.

... Oh, we may collide—and we will do so wholeheartedly! Who knows? We may discover we are soulmates—searching, struggling, changing, and cherishing parts of the tradition we can share.... We may find the Church, reform the Church, be ourselves reformed, conformed, informed by a Christ whose form may surprise us.[13]

June 28: Spiritual disease, sin, evil—call the problem what you will—is rooted in misplaced authority. Each person must struggle between turning herself—her soul—over to others and accepting the essential responsibility for living her own life. The demon, whose name is NONBEING NO AUTHORITY NOTHING NO SELF is exorcised when we accept our humanness—our power and our lack of power; our capacity to pick up ourselves and walk, and when we can't, to acknowledge it and ask for help. The autonomous person will know her interdependence, derived from the autonomy and interdependent needs of others. She will be able to ask for and pursue what she needs. She will not have to manipulate, seduce, or pretend that she has no needs. She will know that all others have needs, which they are entitled to pursue; and that it is in autonomous interdependence that the pursuits of all people become a common pursuit. The common pursuit, a holy pursuit of organic human wholeness, is the mission of the Christian Church.

The absolute *terror* with which NONBEING NO AUTHORITY NOTHING NO SELF threatens the human soul is as indescribable as the *ecstasy* of simply being.

From my experience with this evil, I'd say that the battle against it is, like God, an ongoing process for each of us. The journey at times seems long, and the lamb at times seems heavy, and there are many people, institutions, laws, and traditions that would think they were doing me a favor to carry that lamb for me.

June 29: My Esalen soulmate Lee dreamt that when she returned to New York, she discovered that nothing about her had changed, and that this frightened her. I know the feeling. I believe the change is not as much in who we are as in our *awareness* of who we are. I leave Esalen the same person I was a month ago and, at the same time, with a different perception of this person. I feel better.

June 30: Having just boarded a bus in San Francisco. My anger, somewhat mellowed and more appropriately directed; my feelings, released; my body, stronger; my words, often incidental I think, inadequate expressions of what it is I would like to say; my desire for space and aloneness, real and crucial; my movement, freed up a little; my ability to pray, enhanced; my doubts about myself in the Church, significantly dispelled; my anticipation of this upcoming ordination, delightful, and mind-boggling.

July 1/2: Headed toward Laramie, Wyoming. Sunset is exquisite, and in it the desert's browns and grays look golden. Soft blue hills rise in the distance and, behind them, the light shades into coral pink. It's beautiful, and I'm sad. I'm often sad at sunset, a subdued time, in which I feel subdued. It's true, there's a sadness in my eyes. There's a sense in which I am a sad person. How else can I be? Human pain and tragedy—newspapers on this bus informing us of the assassination in Atlanta of Mrs. Martin Luther King, Sr., the wars and the hunger; the prejudices and acts of discrimination; the alienations each of us experience along the way; the hurt that has come to churchpeople and will come to churchpeople; the pathos of being human. It seems to me that sadness is not an option for anyone who feels. It's a given.

July 4: In Kansas City, Missouri. More than halfway home. With Susan Thornton, friend, feminist, Presbyterian minister who knows what I mean: I anticipate the ordination with a combination of disbelief, excitement, and dread. One should not have to dread one's ordination. Then again, we should not have been put into a discriminatory box from which the only exit is considerably less dreadful than remaining where we are. Thank God that this opportunity is ours! We will celebrate another Independence Day this year!

July 7: Charlotte, N.C. I told Bart [my former rector and employer, at St. Martin's] about our plans. He was amazed! He affirmed me and did not judge my intention to participate in the ordination. He wished me blessings and sent me off with love. Bart means a lot to me both personally and professionally. Were he not going abroad soon, I might well have asked him to consider being my clergy presenter. Perhaps it's just as well he's leaving. Would he say "no" if I were to ask him? How hard that would be to hear. My relationship to Bart may be a prototype of the strained support relationships we are likely to experience long after the proposed ordinations. Many who like us personally and who agree that women should be allowed to be ordained priests and bishops will discover that they cannot go against the official position and join us, or support us, in the ordination and its natural aftermath—e.g., the implementation of our priestly ministries. What will this do to us? Bart is an excellent priest and an honest friend. How will all of the Bart Shermans and Carter

Heywards in this Church be able to maneuver our collision courses without badly hurting each other?

July 8: On to Philadelphia tomorrow for a plenary session with the bishops, other clergy and laypeople, and a handful of us women deacons. This time the question is not whether we will do it. The questions are when, where, and who. I feel excited and anxious, stepping into this chaos, into the surfacing of a Church crisis as old as the traditions which have covered it up. I belong there, and God knows where from there. I am probably freer than I think I am. I hope so.

My parents are concerned about what this means, especially for our "vocational futures" in the Church. I don't know what it means for my vocational future in the Episcopal Church, and at some level, I don't care. I do know what it means in terms of viable Christian community, however. Mama and Daddy have asked me to let them know the date and location so that they can be there.

July 9: En route to Philadelphia. At no time have I been as certain that *we are what we think, feel, and do.* To act on our convictions, to "practice what we preach," is a minimum attempt at integration, the bringing together of parts that have belonged together all along.

As the Gospel of John suggests, Jesus of Nazareth—the person, the Jewish male, the carpenter, in all of his historicity and facticity—not only *gave* us signs; he himself *was* a sign, a living symbol pointing towards a less visible and tangible layer of reality. He not only *instituted* what we have come to call "sacraments"; he himself *was* a sacrament, "an outward and visible sign of an inward and spiritual grace." Jesus not only *spoke* in parables; he himself *was* a parable, a word presented to make a point. Jesus not only *told* us and *showed* us the way to live in relationship to God, to sisters and brothers, and to self; he himself *was* the Way, the Truth, and the Life (John 14:6).

In John, we see an identification of the person Jesus with all that he said and did. There is no dichotomy, or split, between the man and the message.

I see this mode of being as profoundly instructive, if risky, for anyone who calls herself Christian. Gestalt therapy centers on the wholistic bringing together of the splits we normally make between ourselves (who we "really are") on the one hand, and what we do, say, or feel on the other hand. Rather than being people who "have" bodies, spirit, feelings, relationships, and who "do" things, we *are* our bodies, feelings, actions, and so forth. The healthier and better integrated a person is, the less she will experience a split between who she is and the things she does and says.

Or so it seems to me. And so it seemed to the gathering of people in the DeWitt living room who had decided to live into our convictions on the matter of "women's ordination." We found among us an unflappable determination to proceed toward an ordination on July 29, the Feast Day of Mary and Martha.

We were not a fearless group, and we shared our fears about the chaos that would surely ensue. We knew that people would journey from all parts of the nation to celebrate with us. We knew that others would feel wounded, personally attacked, embittered, or outraged. We knew that still others would be unwilling to join us and would privately and absently enjoy the ordination as a symbol of their own liberation. Most Episcopalians, we realized, would be puzzled. They would not understand what was happening, and why.

We could do little about the wounded and embittered except relate to them honestly and responsibly, hoping that on the other side of the steep and rugged mountain, we might together find a common path on which to journey.

We could do little about the quiet and camouflaged supporters except recognize in them our own humanity.

The best we could do for the bewildered in the Church was to proceed with our plans and let education emerge from the ordination itself and its aftermath.

We would notify our own parishes and diocesan bishops immediately. We would inform all bishops, standing committees, and other church leaders shortly before the ordination. We would alert the press approximately twenty-four hours beforehand, so that the general public would know what was happening and so that those within reasonable distance could be with us if they so desired. We would tell our families and close confidants as soon as we wanted to. Otherwise, "mum" would be the word, primarily for security reasons.

I left the Philadelphia meeting on July 10, knowing that, God willing, women deacons would be ordained priests in two and a half weeks. I believed that God was not only willing, but the Prime Mover in the process. Within the days and weeks that were to follow, I would discover a community of people throughout the world who shared this belief.

For the next week and a half, I worked on a syllabus for the fall semester course I would be teaching at Union, "Feminism and Vocation," in which spiritual dimensions of one's "call" and fundamental dynamics of the women's movement would be examined together. Basically, it was to be a course on the spirituality which undergirds people's efforts to be who they are created to be. The summer was an experiential offering in preparation for this course.

Marie Moorefield, Emily Hewitt, and I had wired Bishop Paul Moore, who was vacationing in Europe. We had placed a call to him as well and waited for him to return it. Paul Moore was finally able to reach Emily and to convey his shock that we were planning to take this step; nonetheless, his wish for blessings upon us. Several days later, each of us received a letter from Suffragan Bishop Stuart Wetmore and a "personal and confidential" letter from Paul Moore. Both men, considered strong supporters of women's ordination in principle, asked us to reconsider our intentions, and Bishop Moore officially admonished us not to proceed.

Dear Paul:

I received today your official "admonition" of my plans to be ordained on July 29. I accept this and can understand what you might be feeling, given your position. Each of these days is a day of prayer for me, seeking the guidance of the Holy Spirit.

At this point I do intend to be ordained as scheduled. If I am hereby breaking rank with the discipline of the church, as you indicate, I believe that I am keeping rank with the doctrine of the Church—that Jesus Christ lived, died, and rose for all persons and that the orders of his ministry are to reflect this grace. I believe that the time for this is, and always will be, now. . . .

Faithfully,
Carter

My rector, Neale Secor, was considering presenting me for ordination. He was concerned not at all about whether or not the ordination was right. Like the majority of people in the parish, he was unambivalent in his knowledge that this should happen and that it should happen now. Neale was concerned, however, about the consequences this event might heap upon the parish itself. After struggling with the dilemma for several days, Neale decided to join us in Philadelphia—officially, as Emily's and my rector, and as my clergy presenter. His wife, Christine, was to be Emily's lay presenter.

There are few people to whom I have been closer than Betty Mosley, a friend at Union, at the time a counselor to women at Columbia University, and the wife of Bishop Brooke Mosley. I had come to know the Mosleys while he was president of Union Seminary. Betty had been an ardent and active supporter of women's ordination. Moreover, she had shown me the extent to which this was an issue for *all* women, not just those seeking ordination.

Time and again, at lunch, late at night, at meetings, walking down Broadway, Betty and I had empathized with each other as each sought to live into her respective vocation in Church, seminary, and society at large. We had seen that the hurdles before us were similar, if not identical. And we had been able to give each other support as we went about the business of leaping over external expectations of the roles we "should" be playing—bishop's wife, woman deacon, president's wife, female seminarian, Episcopal lady, single girl, mother, hostess, daughter, female citizen in a male's world. Betty Mosley enthusiastically agreed to fly to Philadelphia from their summer parish on Buzzard's Bay in order to present me for ordination to the priesthood.

> *I have renewed hope that the church might yet be a place where I could raise a daughter in good conscience and experience a full life myself. By your courage, you have given a great deal to the church, and I, as a recipient, am very, very grateful to you."*
> —Letter to me from laywoman,
> Diocese of West Virginia, spring, 1975.

About ten days before the ordination, I mailed out some fifteen invitations to friends I had not been able to reach by phone or in person. Responses returned rapidly. From Tom F. Driver, professor of theology at Union: "I'm amazed! In this instance it seems to be amazing grace." From Bob Handy, professor of Church history at Union: "Knowing a little of your pilgrimage, I know how important this occasion is for you—and for all of us." From Lee Hancock, seminarian: "Please know I am with you. I send you energy from the West." John Lowick, Episcopal priest: "I'm as excited by this as by anything that has ever happened in the Church. Bless all of you for taking this tremendous leap. I'll be there." And from Vic, Esalen brother and Roman Catholic priest: "*Love is sharing a priesthood.*"

To our surprise, the news hit the press on July 20. Within twelve hours, our phones had begun ringing in tempo with the traffic light changes on the corner outside my office. A press release had been prepared for July 28, not before. We had agreed, however, that in the event the news were to break prematurely, we would offer "no comment." We believed that the

Philadelphia ordination would speak for itself; that the action would be stronger than any words with which we might attempt to explain it. There would be ample opportunity to meet the press, the public and many brother and sister Episcopalians after the fact.

I spent the last few days leading up to July 29 fending off the calls of well-meaning press people; answering correspondence from Episcopalians who had written to convey delight, disgust, bewilderment, or confidence; and helping plan, with Nancy Wittig, a retreat to be held at the DeWitt home, on July 28, for ordinands, bishops, family, and friends.

Then, on Friday, July 26, I took off for Putney, Vermont, where a gathering of intimates had long been scheduled. We shared two days—singing, dancing, and speculating every now and then in anticipation of the upcoming ordination, to which most of the group would be traveling.

Among the most elated, and deeply moved, at the thought of July 29 was Bev Harrison, my friend who had once upon a time watched me sink into despair precisely because I could not seem to stand on my own two feet and walk, as a churchwoman, as a female person.

The Vermont cabin belongs in part to Leslie, wise and gentle pragmatist, innovative head of a New York school. Leslie *was* an Episcopalian. For all practical purposes, she is now an "Episcopal alumna," having left the church. As the rest of us sat marveling that women would be ordained *priests* on Monday, Leslie offered a wry suggestion, "You know, they really ought to be consecrating a few *bishops*."

Now the eleven disciples went to Galilee, to the mountain to which Jesus had directed them. And when they saw him they worshiped him; but some doubted. And Jesus came and said to them, "All authority in heaven and on earth has been given to me. Go therefore and make disciples of all nations, baptizing them in the name of the Father and of the Son and of the Holy Spirit,

teaching them to observe all that I have commanded you; and lo, I
am with you always, to the close of the age."

Matthew 28:16-20

When Bishop Edward G. Welles II prays, one has the feeling
that the Lord is bound to take notice. With him as celebrant,
some one hundred people made our communion on the lawn as
the July 28 sun began to disappear from the skies over Ambler,
Pennsylvania. Mrs. Welles, her ordinand-daughter Katrina
Welles Swanson, Katrina's priest-husband George, and their sons
William and Olof sat near the middle of a semicircle that had
formed to worship and to reflect. None of the Welles or Swan-
sons needed actually to say anything. Their faces said it all. Here
were people for whom the Lord is unmistakably central. No one
among us had struggled more earnestly with whether or not to
participate in the ordination than Bishop Welles, who in fact
continued to ponder his place in this process. Yet no one among
us was clearer in his or her affect that this was just about the
greatest and most Spirit-filled occasion in the life of the Episcopal Church. When William Swanson was asked why he had
come, he answered proudly, "I've come to see my mother ordained
to the priesthood and I hope my grandfather will do it."

Our corporate body's pulse beat joy! As ambivalent and anxious as most had been, we were amazed, even eager. I had only
to catch seventy-nine-year-old Jeannette Piccard's sparkling eyes,
manifesting her recognition of a destination toward which she
had been journeying since her call at age eleven, to know that
all was well.

People mingled leisurely for several hours. My father and Bill
Schiess, husband of ordinand Betty, stood laughing on the porch,
perhaps reflecting their release from the absurdity with which
each of them had viewed this dilemma all along. Methodist minister Rich Wittig, Nancy's husband, expressed colorfully his
opinion of the Episcopal Church's treatment of his wife—and
himself. Several people were startled by his frankness; nearly all
of us knew what he meant. Others milled, nibbling on chicken

wings, drinking wine, marveling: My mother; Elizabeth and Bishop Dan Corrigan; Neale and Christine Secor; Ann Smith from Philadelphia, who had helped organize the retreat; Mary Sue Willie and her husband Charles, our preacher; Paul Washington, rector of the Church of the Advocate, hosting the ordination; Jane Lynch, my childhood friend and church organist from Charlotte, N.C.; spouses, siblings, children, parents, nieces, nephews, rectors, colleagues, and close friends. This was no less a community celebration than a wedding—except in this case there were many principal characters whose lives were being altered irreversibly.

Not too late into the evening, our friends dispersed, leaving three bishops and eleven ordinands to our retreat. Dan Corrigan reflected with us about the priesthood. Alla Bozarth-Campbell made a spirited entry into this discussion, expressing a firm conviction that she had come to Philadelphia in order for an Episcopal body of the faithful to recognize and confirm what is *already* an "ontological" reality—i.e., a reality at the deepest level of her being: her participation in the priesthood of Christ.

Dan Corrigan sat back, folded his hands in his lap, and smiled, "Yes, in the ways of God—ontologically—you are already priests; you have always been priests; and you will always be priests." Ecclesiastically, which is to say, for all practical purposes in the life of the Church, we were to "be made priests" the following day.

Each bishop then met with the women he had examined and intended to ordain. Emily, Marie, and I sat and talked with Bob DeWitt, discussing how we felt about what was happening. We believed that we were as ready as people would ever be for ordination to the priesthood. Bob said he was amazed at us. We said we were amazed at him. All of us were amazed at ourselves and at everything else.

The bishops signed the Bibles which were to be given to us during the service and asked us to bring them with us to the church. We agreed to meet the next morning as soon after nine as possible in order to dodge crowds and find quiet time together.

As excited as we were, we knew we needed to go home to sleep.

As we were preparing to leave, Bishop Tony Ramos walked in the front door. He grinned.

The choir room at the Church of the Advocate was just large enough to accommodate fifteen people. Every several minutes, one of us would be called out to greet a friend or receive a gift or message—from Missouri, California, Ohio, Virginia, Canada, New York, England, Ireland, South Africa. The Secors had presented Emily and me with heavy, simple, attractive silver crosses. A Roman Catholic priest from Dayton, Ohio, had sent his cross to be worn by any one of us; Doris Mote, a deacon from Southern Ohio had given it to Katrina. Philadelphia friends had made Sue a stole for the occasion, and Bishop Welles had offered her another. Flowers arrived for Alison from her husband Bruce.

By 10:30 A.M. each of us had vested in her alb and was busy learning how to loop and knot the cincture. Each bishop was vesting in the manner in which he was most comfortable. Minutes before the service, we gathered for the taking and signing of the Oath of Conformity, which we believed required rather than inhibited our ordination.

Jeannette had pointed out that "discipline" is rooted in the word "disciple," and that a disciple is one who follows when Christ calls.

Even those of us who viewed the "discipline of the Church" as something of a stumbling block to the manner in which we were to be ordained recognized that godly "doctrine" made the ordination imperative. We believed ourselves faced with a choice between "discipline" and "doctrine." Time and again we must make decisions. We had made ours. We prayed that the Holy Spirit might fill the service, and we headed up the spiral staircase to await the beginning of the ordination.

Barely audible to us as we lined the wall of the sacristy and hall was the voice of rector Paul Washington, "We are all . . . acutely and painfully aware of the fact that the Holy Spirit has compelled us to act at a time which is considered by some to be untimely.... What is one to do when the democratic process, the political dynamics, and the legal guidelines are out of step with the Divine Imperative which says 'Now is the time'? What is a mother to do when the doctor says, 'Your baby will be born on August 10th,' when on July 29 she has reached the last stages of labor pains and the water sack has ruptured?" Seconds later the processional began: "Come, Labor On."

Laughing, we began to move slowly in toward the nave. Smiling, we nodded in salutation to several scores of our brother and sister clergy, vested and ready to fall in with us. An assortment of Episcopal clerics ranging from women deacons to retired priests reached out to us as we passed.

Approaching the door to the nave, my eyes began to pop. There was no aisle, no room to walk. Well over a thousand, maybe two thousand, people were pressed in close to participate. The path to the chancel area cleared itself as we moved steadily, if timidly, on through jubilant hellos, waves, hugs, flash bulbs, and television cameras moving with us.

When Bishops Corrigan, DeWitt, Ramos, and Welles stepped through the door, applause burst forth so resoundingly as to fill the space around and within us. The foundations of the Church seemed to tremble. I myself began to tremble. Tears ran down my cheeks as I turned in exclamation to Betty Mosley, "Incredible!"

When at last we were seated, Charles Willie, black educator and at the time vice-president of the Episcopal Church's House of Deputies, was ushered to the pulpit:

> The hour cometh and now is, when the true worshipers shall worship God in spirit and in truth. This is the hour of truth....
>
> I participate in this service today not because I wanted to speak out but because I could not remain silent....
>
> Twice during the 1970 decade, the General Convention was presented the opportunity to confirm the personhood of women by affirming their right to be professional priests. Twice it did blunder. Some might say that the actions of General Convention were not sexist and had nothing to do with discrimination against women.

At her ordination to the priesthood, Episcopal deacon Carter Heyward flanked by her lay and clergy presenters, Betty Mosley and Neale Secor, enters the Church of the Advocate in Philadelphia, July 29, 1974.

But I say that an overwhelming majority of General Convention members are men. This fact speaks louder than their denial of the presence of prejudice....

There is a dictum in American jurisprudence that justice delayed is justice denied....

There are parallels between the Civil Rights Movement and the Women's Movement and this is what we are witnessing today. In reality, both are freedom movements for men as well as women, and for blacks and browns as well as whites. Unfulfilled hope tends to turn into despair and eventually into rage....

As blacks refused to participate in their own oppression by going to the back of the bus in 1955 in Montgomery, women are refusing to cooperate in their own oppression by remaining on the periphery of full participation in the Church in 1974 in Philadelphia....

God grant that the Church may see the true mission of women as it is meant to be. Here we stand to stake our claim and our version of truth as we understand it, that all believers are priests in the kingdom of God and have a right to full participation in the affairs of Church and society. And we also vow to make no peace with oppression, whether it is sexism or racism. We can do nothing else, so help us God. With God's help, we shall overcome. AMEN.

Intermittently throughout the sermon, the congregation roared its affirmation.

In unison, our presenters spoke to the bishops, "Reverend Father in God, I present unto you these persons present, to be admitted to the Order of Priesthood." One by one, our names were listed. There followed the prescribed chance for any person to "come forth in the Name of God" to make known any "crime or impediment" because of which the ordinands should not be received into "this holy Ministry."

Five male priests stepped forward to address the congregation, and principals, on such "impediments" as canonical interpretation against the ordination of women; the "perversion" implicit in any attempt to ordain a woman priest (like attempting to change "stones to bread"; emitting the "smell, sight, and sound of perversion"); Jeannette Piccard's being "too old" to be priested; and the ordination's timing being premature—i.e., prior to the next General Convention. Paul Washington smiled and thanked the protesters for having expressed themselves. He then turned to Bishop Corrigan, who for the bishops, responded to the charges of impediment:

Our common dilemma is presented at the outset by the requirement that each ordinand, first, declare her belief that the Holy Scriptures of the Old and New Testaments contain all things necessary to salvation; secondly, take the canonical Oath of Conformity to the doctrine, discipline, and worship of the Protestant Episcopal Church in the United States of America; and thirdly, make a similar liturgical promise placed in the ordinal.

The conflict between both revelation in the Scriptures and the doctrine of the Church, on the one hand, and the discipline, rules, and regulations and common practices of the Protestant Episcopal Church on the other hand, have long been both observed and experienced.

There is nothing new in being compelled to choose the truth revealed in Scripture and expressed in doctrine when this truth is in conflict with our rules and ways.

This is such a time. Neither the Word nor the great expositions of that Word forbid what we propose. Indeed, that which both declare about women in creation and in the new creation command our present action. The time for our obedience is now!

The litany was made; the collect prayed; and the Epistle read by Kate Mead, widow of Delaware's late Bishop William Mead who had hoped to plan and participate in this very ordination. Pat Park, who had not been a deacon long enough to be ordained a priest with us (minimum requirement of time, six months), read to us from the Gospel of Matthew.

When Jesus saw the multitudes, he was moved with compassion on them, because they fainted, and were scattered abroad as sheep having no shepherd. Then saith he unto his disciples, "The harvest truly is plenteous, but the labourers are few; pray ye therefore the Lord of the harvest, that he will send forth labourers into his harvest".

Matthew 9:36–38, KJV

The eleven of us moved to the altar rail where we were given our charge. We took our vows and knelt for the *Veni, Creator Spiritus* ("Come, Holy Ghost"), hymn in which the Spirit is invoked.

Each of the three ordaining bishops was to ordain the women he had known best, examined, or otherwise believed he should ordain. Within these sets of three, we would be ordained according to our seniority in the diaconate.

Daniel Corrigan and his friend of many years, Jeannette Piccard—who, he had noted, ought to be ordaining him—stepped to the top of the chancel stairs. The bishop sat down and the majestic deacon, flanked by her three sons and her aging clergy presenter Denzil Carty from Minnesota, knelt at his feet. There followed Alla, Betty, and Merrill. Possibly a hundred Episcopal and Roman Catholic priests had gathered close to participate in the laying-on-of-hands, the rite which signifies a person's ordination at the hands of the Church.

Bishop Corrigan rose and offered his place to Bishop DeWitt. Emily was ordained; then, Marie. As Marie stepped back, I stepped forward, catching the bishop's eye momentarily, and as if strangely transcendent of the time at hand, my whole life seemed contained within the moment: past, present, future. All that had ever mattered to me flooded within me, as a geyser of lifeblood or holy water.

Whatever "authority problems" with which I had victimized myself in the past, or would give myself over to in the future, vanished in the present glimpse of God's holy community, both here now and always coming.

On my own two feet I stood there, supported by a congregation of faithful friends and strangers who had come on their own. Among them was my therapist, Arthur, who, following Bob, had worked with me for years, encouraging me to grasp life in my own hands and use it. Among them were others who had helped shape my ministry and I theirs, all of us yearning for community in which we could live more fully and freely into our potentials as sisters and brothers, one in Christ.

On my own feet, I stood there, a member of the Church of God, an Episcopal deacon, a willing ordinand for the priesthood which Sophie Couch had authoritatively acknowledged as hers more than twenty years before.

And on my knees, I knelt before a person who had always assured me that God breaks into our lives in surprising ways when we least expect it, empowering us with the authority to move with the Spirit into new places. I bowed my head, and the weight of the Church bore down upon me. Bishop DeWitt held my head firmly and touched my soul as he spoke:

Take thou Authority to execute the Office of a Priest in the Church of God, now committed to thee by the Imposition of our hands. And be thou a faithful Dispenser of the Word of God, and of his holy Sacraments; In the name of the Father, and of the Son, and of the Holy Ghost. Amen.

Soon after her ordination as a deacon, Carter Heyward and Bishop J. Brooke Mosley dance together in the filming of a movie about Union Theological Seminary at New York City Hall, Fall, 1973.

I rose to participate in the faithful dispensation of the Holy Order of Priesthood, as my sisters Sue, Katrina, Alison, and Nancy knelt to receive it.

During the communion which followed, person upon person asked us for blessings. I placed my hands on the head of a friend and spoke of a peace which passes all understanding.

> *You've had your way—Great! Squeeze every glorious moment out of it. Actually, you're just playing games. After all, your church's founder, Henry VIII, was no more obedient than you and no more pleasing to Almighty God!*
>   —Letter to me from Roman Catholic laywoman,
>   California, summer, 1974.

On August 1, Bishop Paul Moore phoned me. He had returned that day from his trip to Europe and wanted to hear about the ordination. Paul noted that, while he wished he could have been present for it, he knew that even if he had been in the States, he could not have participated. He then asked me to agree *not* to exercise my priesthood "for the time being." The two of us concurred that either of us could step out of the agreement at any time.

Several days later, I received a note from Paul, recording the gist of the agreement we had reached on the phone. He stated in his letter that he wanted time to discuss the situation with both the Standing Committee of the Diocese and the House of Bishops, the latter having been called to a special meeting two weeks hence.

On August 8, a letter was mailed from the Bishop to all clergy in the Diocese of New York. This letter conveyed Paul Moore's instructions: (1) that Emily, Marie, and I refrain from exercising priesthood "until further notice" and (2) that all rectors and other ecclesiastical authorities in the diocese refrain from inviting us to serve as priests.

I had agreed to refrain from all *public* priestly ministry *only* until Paul had been able to consult with the Standing Committee and the House of Bishops. I felt, as did my sister priests, that our own dioceses needed time to ascertain how they might best open themselves officially to the ministries we offered.

I celebrated several private House Communions, the first with my own family and old friends at home. And I waited to see what would happen next in the public arenas of Episcopal reaction to women priests.

What a great encouragement it is for me, an orthodox Jewish woman who's been working for some time toward some long-overdue changes in Jewish law and attitudes regarding women, to see other religious women within an authoritarian religious community take REAL *action to improve their situation, without having to step outside the tradition completely.*

—Letter to me from Jewish woman,
New York City, summer, 1974.

Many people wonder why we could not have waited longer for approval of a General Convention, for permission from our diocesan bishops, for support of most Episcopalians, for some gesture, or event, or time in near or distant future in which some agreement might be reached that women can be priests of the Church of God.

The Church hierarchy is bothered by you now, but it wasn't bothered at all last year at General Convention, when it voted for brutality to women, called its vote a fluke, and declared the subject closed for the next three years. Courage! The nation endorsed morality last week; perhaps our church may too.

—Letter to me from laywoman,
Diocese of North Carolina, summer, 1974.

On August 14, 1974, Episcopal bishops from all over the United States rushed to Chicago for an emergency meeting, called by Presiding Bishop Allin for the specific purpose of responding to the Philadelphia service.

Nine of the eleven new priests flew to Chicago, too, for the purposes of being available, should the bishops wish to speak to us about our vocations, and of observing the proceedings.

The House of Bishops (the official gathering of Episcopal bishops) met for two days. We stood alongside, watching and listening. Together with other Episcopalians, who had come to observe, we were unacknowledged and treated as if we were invisible. We, however, knew well how visible and clear our presence was among the bishops.

The bishops sought some way of condemning their brothers who had ordained us, and of invalidating our ordinations, without appearing to be Pharisaic legalists. They finally produced a resolution that contained a little love, a little vindication, a little anguish, a little soft brutality, a little pastoral concern, and a little legalism.

FINAL REPORT OF THE COMMITTEE ON RESOLUTIONS
[HOUSE OF BISHOPS, AUGUST 15, 1974]

The House of Bishops in no way seeks to minimize the genuine anguish that so many in the Church feel at the refusal to date of the Church to grant authority for women to be considered as Candidates for Ordination to the Priesthood and Episcopacy. Each of us in his own way shares in that anguish. Neither do we question the sincerity of the motives of the four Bishops and eleven Deacons who acted as they did in Philadelphia. Yet in God's work, ends and means must be consistent with one another. Furthermore, the wrong means to reach a desired end may expose the Church to serious consequences unforeseen and undesired by anyone.

Whereas our Lord has called us to walk the way of the Cross through the questions and issues before us resulting from the service in Philadelphia on July 29th, 1974, and

Whereas the Gospel compels us to be as concerned with equality, freedom, justice and reconciliation and above all love, as with the order of our common life and the exercise of legitimate authority, therefore, be it

Resolved, that the House of Bishops, having heard from Bishops Corrigan, DeWitt, Welles and Ramos, the reasons for their action, express our understanding of their feelings and concern, but express our disagreement with acting in violation of the collegiality of the House of Bishops, as well as the legislative process of the whole Church.

Further, we express our conviction that the necessary conditions for valid ordination to the Priesthood in the Episcopal Church were not fulfilled on the occasion in question; since we are convinced that a bishop's authority to ordain can be effectively exercised only in and for a community which has authorized him to act for them, and as a member of the Episcopal College; and since there was a failure to act in fulfillment of constitutional and canonical requirements for ordination, and be it further

Resolved, that we believe it is urgent that the General Convention reconsider at the Minneapolis meeting [next meeting of General Convention, September, 1976] the question of the Ordination of Women to the Priesthood, and be it

Resolved, that this House call upon all concerned to wait upon and abide by whatever action the General Convention decides upon in this regard.

There was no discussion of this motion. The voting simply began. As the voting came to its *end*, a bishop stood up and asked the presiding bishop what the resolution meant.

"Does it mean the ladies are not priests?"

The presiding bishop assured him that the ordinations were, in fact, "invalid"—that the ladies were indeed *not* priests.

A number of bishops then jumped up to change their votes from "aye" to "abstain" or from "abstain" to "no." The Bishop of New York was one such bishop, who, in the final analysis, chose to abstain rather than vote yes or no.

The motion passed: yes—128; no—9; abstain—10; and Charles Willie thereupon resigned as vice-president of the House of Deputies, protesting what he called the bishops' "display of blatant male chauvinism."

Parable: August 15, 1974

Pushing his way through the darkness, the King pursued IT. All his life he had been taught that he must be ready for IT. Whatever IT was, IT would destroy him.

The summer had seemed longer and hotter than usual. The

people had seemed restless and anxious. Troubled, the King had been pacing the halls when the word reached him. "IT is nearing the castle!" Frantically, in defense of the castle, which he had been taught to recognize as defense of the people, the King grabbed his heavy purple shield and the silver sword which had been given him by the people. He scurried into the courtyard, mounted his horse, and rode off into the night to find IT.

The air was thicker than usual, the mountains steeper than he had remembered them, and the forest seemed to him a maze, as if he had never been there before. He spurred his horse, stiffened his jaws, and charged on, as if IT were a matter of life and death.

His anger at ITS audacity became more prominent the further into the maze he rode. What was IT? Where was IT? Although he had been warned often of ITS danger, no one had ever been able to tell him what IT looked like. Come to think of it, no one had ever told him what IT wanted. As he thought about IT, he became frightened.

He bore the prongs of his heels into the ribs of his horse and struck the beast such a blow that he found himself sitting in the midst of a thicket. Slightly bruised, he sat dazed, only to listen as his horse galloped into the night. His eyes began to scan the brush. He could not see! But he knew—his sword was gone.

"To hell with IT!" he shouted to himself, and his thoughts turned to the disquieting task of returning safely to the castle on foot. He must journey back without encountering IT. In frustration, he beat his fist on what he assumed was ground and instead made solid contact with metal. "My shield!" he exclaimed. "At least I can protect myself from IT."

Painstakingly he picked himself up, shield in hand, and began a long, slow limp in some direction. He was tired, but he dared not sleep, lest IT catch him by surprise.

All at once, he heard IT. He could not tell from which direction, but he heard IT. IT was nearby. IT sounded like a bird, but the King did not believe that birds could sing in the night. IT was against the law of nature.

"Where are you?" he shouted.

"In front of you," came the reply, somewhat less melodiously than one might expect from a bird.

"*What* are you?" the King demanded.

"I am a bird."

The King was more annoyed than frightened. He squinted in the direction of the voice and spoke loudly, "Birds do not sing in the night. You are *not* a bird. I will ask you again, and I will expect the truth, for I am a King. What exactly are you?"

"I know you are a King, and I know I am a bird." The voice was surprisingly stern, then somewhat softer, "Why are you troubled?"

The King was abashed. He had no inclination to admit that, in search of IT, he was lost in the forest. "Tell me," he demanded, "have you ever heard of IT?"

"What?" the voice inquired.

"IT!" the King retorted indignantly. He did not like to appear unclear about anything.

"You are not making sense to me," the bird replied, as graciously as a bird can reply to a King.

"You impudent creature!" he screamed, flailing his shield furiously in the direction of the voice. "I could smash you with this shield, and I will do so unless you tell me how you sing in the night, if you are a bird, and why, regardless of what you are, you were presumptuous enough to bother me as I strolled through the forest tonight!"

"Birds sing—day or night. That you do not ordinarily hear us is beside the point. We are not bound by the laws of nature you have established with which to understand us. We did not make these laws and you did not consult us when you made them. We sing whenever there is someone around who can appreciate our voices."

"You do not realize how you enrage me! Be gone at once!" the King commanded.

"I thought that perhaps you needed me," suggested the stubborn voice.

"Arghhh!" The King hurled his shield directly at the voice which he had come to hate, and he was immediately alarmed because he knew he had lost that with which he could protect himself from IT. "Szzechhh!" he snarled and stumbled on through the forest, as if he knew where he were going.

Never had he known such despair. No sword. No shield. No one. Not even a sense of direction. And IT could be lurking anywhere, watching him, waiting to devour him. Hours, days, passed. He lumbered on.

Finally, too discouraged to be frightened any more, he sat down. His head lowered and his eyes fastened catatonically downward, he saw something he could not believe: There, in front of him, rusty and purple, lay his shield—and in it, a nest of weed and bramble.

"Hello!" came the familiar voice.

Unable to believe his ears, he lifted his eyes, and there, perched in a high branch of the tree, sat what looked to him like a bird, its head cocked, waiting for response.

"I didn't hurt you?" asked the subdued King.

"No, birds can fly as well as sing!" she assured him, and flew up a branch in demonstration of her escape.

The King bowed his head. "I'm glad. You see, you—uh, IT—IT had frightened me terribly, and I was beside myself with strange feelings." He paused, embarrassed, then asked abashedly, "By any chance, do you know how I might get out of here?"

"Yes," the bird nodded towards the thickest part of the forest and the steep mountain which framed it. "I can go along with you."

The King was taken aback. Why would a creature whom he had attempted to kill make such an offer? He bit his lip and looked skeptically up at her. "I don't know," he mused aloud. "For all I know, you'll lead me to IT! For all I know you *are* IT!"

Her small wings pressed in close to her back, her head cocked purposefully, her sharp black eyes penetrating the space between them, her narrow legs braced like steel on the limb above, she puzzled him. Her presence was both fearful and comforting.

When at last she spoke, she spoke slowly, "If you want me to accompany you, I will. If not, I will journey on alone and you can do as you please. But you will stand a better chance of making it home if I am with you. *Because you are lost, and, for the time being, I am not.*"

A deep silence fell between them.

With some cautious hesitancy, the King sighed his consent. He reached for his heavy purple shield. Curiously, he lifted the brambled twigs out of the center as if to take the nest along. He glanced at the bird who nodded her affirmation.

As they journeyed, the air seemed to clear. The forest and the mountains seemed less tedious. In order to carry the nest without snapping its sticks and bits, the King had dispensed with the shield in a cluster of berry bushes. He fantasized a homecoming among the people. He felt more like their brother, less like their King.

On one peculiarly difficult day, as he squeezed through thorns fastened well into crevices along the mountain slope, he found himself anxious about IT. But the bird soared, beckoning him home.

Any attempt to postpone justice is a sign of weak faith. The fearful hullabaloo among Episcopal bishops—their fear of schism, of alienating powerful churchpeople, of ecclesiastical trials, of their own loss of good standing, of throwing their dioceses into chaos, of us—suggests to me that these people, taken as a collegium (which is how they have asked to be taken), do not have faith that the Holy Spirit will move where it will move. The Church will be what it will be. Yahweh said, "I WILL BE WHAT I WILL BE." Christians are charged to believe this, without knowing just where we are going, yet knowing that it will always be a just way—and that it will always be *now*.

Dear Paul:

I write with a heavy heart in response to the action taken yesterday by the House of Bishops. Women with me in Chicago, and women elsewhere, stand together appalled at the bishops' hardened, sexist resolution whereby our ordinations were deemed invalid. That the resolution was steeped in language of love and concern suggests to me only the depth, pathos, and tragedy of our brothers' inability to relate to us as sisters. Lining the walls and halls, we were strangely invisible. Had there been any question in my mind that the July 29 ordination was inappropriate, witnessing the House of Bishops would have erased all doubt.... As of today, August 16, 1974, I end my agreement not to exercise priestly functions "until further notice." . . .

Sincerely,
Carter

Paul's response followed quickly. He, too, was hurt—"traumatized," he said—by the House of Bishops. He was, however, disturbed that I had decided to end our agreement. He told me that any priestly activities on my part would only contribute to the already existent confusion about the ordinations, and he warned that he might have to discipline me in some yet undetermined way. At the same time, he sent his good wishes and affection.

Having voted for the resolution in Chicago, I find that I am in contradiction with myself, and I must recognize the fact that your orders, though highly irregular—which I am sure you recognize— are certainly valid.... I would like you to accept my apology for voting the way I did in Chicago.
—Letter to me from diocesan bishop,
Province VII (Southwest), summer, 1974.

It will always be true that we see now through a glass darkly what we shall see someday face to face. Catching only hazy glimpses of God's glory in which we live, and toward which we move, we must either act now—and it is *always* now—or confess that we are not alive in the moment and cannot go with God into new places today. Maybe tomorrow.

I trust that nothing will ever dilute or diminish the joy that has been radiating from your face in the pictures the papers have had of you. . . . Aren't indelible marks wonderful?
                    —Letter to me from Roman Catholic priest,
                    North Carolina, summer, 1974.

Realizing that, technically, one is granted a "license" before functioning as a priest, albeit an automatic process within one's own diocese, I wrote to the bishop, requesting this license.

Dear Paul:

I am writing to ask that I be licensed as a priest in the Diocese of New York. As you know, I believe that such positive action on the parts of the diocesan bishops who have women priests is both appropriate and far more regular than the action the bishops took in Chicago. . . .

                                        Sincerely,
                                        Carter

The bishop's reply was brief: No. He could not, or would not, license me. And he suggested that I knew well why not.

Be assured of my continual intercession on behalf of you and your sister-priests.
                    —Letter to me from Anglican laywoman,
                    Quebec, Canada, fall, 1974.

I regret that I must cancel your invitation to come to this church to preach. . . . In pursuing ordination to the priesthood contrary to the laws and will of the Episcopal Church, you are separating yourself from the Body of Christ.
                    —Letter to me from priest,
                    Diocese of Western New York, summer, 1974.

I have thought and prayed over the matter of whether or not I, as an individual, will consider these ordinations valid. I find them extremely shaky, but my own theology demands that I recognize

*them as valid. Therefore, when next we meet, I will truly be able to
vent my anger with you by addressing you as "The Reverend
Mother Fucker!"*

—Letter to me from priest,
Diocese of Dallas, summer, 1974.

In October, 1974, New York's three women priests and three
women deacons met, at our request, with both the bishop and the
Standing Committee in order to restate our requests that we
priests be licensed and that the deacons be ordained to the
priesthood, without further delay.

The Standing Committee's reaction to us seemed to be that we
should keep up our insistence if we really believed in what we're
doing, and that no one—yea, not even the Standing Committee
itself—should be able to stop us.

What I recall most vividly from this meeting was that the
windows in the large Gothic room all blew open at once when
one of the women clergy mentioned the Holy Spirit.

Shortly thereafter, Paul Moore attended the regular annual
meeting of the House of Bishops, this time in Oaxtepec, Mexico.
As the bishops were edging toward a retraction of their Chicago
statement on the "invalidity" of the ordinations, and were con-
jecturing that the ordinations might be "completable" at some
point in the (far distant) future, we ourselves were busy planning our first public celebration of the Holy Eucharist—as valid,
complete priests. Word of our plans appeared in the Mexican
press, as elsewhere, and I received another letter from Paul
Moore in which he expressed his regret that I continued to heap
bitterness upon myself by my attitude and actions.

*Snickers, chuckles, and guffaws, by Baptist, Adventists, Pente-
costals, Lutherans, and other religious groups greeted your ordination to a spurious priesthood. . . . Why don't you start your own*

church, name it St. Feminist, and promote yourself to the first
Bishopric? You will give the people another laugh.
—Letter to me from man,
Forest Hills, New York, summer, 1974.

Dear Paul:
You said that you are sorry that I "keep doing things that
needlessly exacerbate bitterness" against me . . . , furthermore that
it's quite unnecessary and that if I would just quit "doing things,"
the problem would resolve itself . . . and we could live together as
one, whole, Christian family. But like grace, reconciliation is not
so cheap. The reality of our Church is that it is split wide open. . . .
The signs of the times are ones of struggle—only then, of reconciliation. Anger and bitterness are to be expected. . . .
Sincerely, and fondly,
Carter

You are all egotists and a discredit to our church.
—Letter to me from laywoman,
Diocese of Arizona, fall, 1974.

Paul wrote back, assuring me that *he* was not bitter and that, in
fact, he admired greatly the three women from New York who
had been ordained in Philadelphia. He offered his concern about
me, given the tension he imagined I was having to bear. And he
sent his warm greetings.

Having been a lifelong Episcopalian, it pains me, to say the least,
to have to contemplate leaving the church, but that is exactly what
I am thinking over at this point. It strikes me that as difficult as it is
to be a Christian in the world, it is more difficult to be a Christian
in the Church. I wonder how many more women feel as I do—
many, I am sure. . . . There is nothing to stop us from having a
home Eucharist with you to celebrate.
—Letter to me from laywoman,
Diocese of Long Island, fall, 1974.

We could have waited—until tomorrow; until 1976; until . . .
we could have waited forever. We did not *have* to do it. We *chose*

to do it. The Lord God of justice always calls people to just action *now*. Usually we do not respond decisively. We do not hear the call, or we do not understand it, or we do not take it seriously, or we are too busy with other priorities. Occasionally, by grace, a human being will *choose* to respond *now*.

I deeply regret the impatience that led the eleven and the four to proceed so hastily. I wish you were free to give yourself to your work with people instead of having to carry the burden that haste has put upon you.

> —Letter to me from laywoman,
> Diocese of Connecticut, fall, 1974.

Thank you for helping us come face to face with our Lord's burning love.

> —Letter to me from diocesan bishop,
> Province VIII (West), summer, 1974

The manner in which you have chosen to end discrimination in our church is correct and proper and anything but civil disobedience and I encourage you to redouble your efforts.

> —Letter to me from layman,
> Diocese of Western North Carolina, fall, 1974.

FOR IMMEDIATE RELEASE—

A Service in Celebration of Women in Ministry will be held on Reformation Sunday, October 27, 1974, at Riverside Church, New York City. Commitment to the creation of this service was generated by representatives from 19 Protestant denominations, Roman Catholic organizations and ecumenical church agencies gathered on October 1 at the first meeting of the Commission on Women in Ministry, Division of Education and Ministry, National Council of Churches. Among the co-sponsors of the service are the following groups:

Chicago Ecumenical Women's Centers
Church Employed Women, United Presbyterian Church
Commission on Women in Ministry, Division of Education
    and Ministry, National Council of Churches

Commission on the Status and Role of Women, United
    Methodist Church
Ministries to Blacks in Higher Education
National Black Sisters' Conference
National Episcopal Women's Caucus
NETWORK
Office of Women's Affairs, Graduate Theological Union,
    Berkeley, California
Philadelphia Task Force on Women in Religion
Riverside Church Women's Center
Women Committed to Women, Los Angeles, California
Women's Division, Board of Global Ministries, United
    Methodist Church
Women in Campus Ministry
Women's Theological Coalition of the Boston Theological
    Institute
Union Theological Seminary Women's Caucus
United Church of Christ Task Force on Women in Church
    and Society
United Presbyterian Council on Women and the Church

In an ecumenical setting, the Eucharist will be celebrated by
three of the Episcopal women priests recently ordained in Philadelphia: The Rev. Carter Heyward, the Rev. Jeannette Piccard,
and the Rev. Alison Cheek. Preaching will be the Rev. Carol
Anderson, an Episcopal deacon. Participants will include other
women deacons, Episcopal male clergy, and women in ministry
from several Protestant denominations and Roman Catholic
groups.

Affirming the wholeness of the Body of Christ, we, the co-
sponsors of this Celebration will lift up the ministry of women in
the churches. The controversy surrounding the ordination of
eleven Episcopal women to the priesthood highlights the dilemma
of all women in all churches: when we are present, we are ignored;
when we speak, we are not heard. So, in this moment of history,
we stand beside our Episcopal sisters, offering them our ministry of
support and solidarity; receiving from them a sacramental ministry
which we affirm as theirs to celebrate. By our action at this service,
the ministry of all women will be made visible, will be heard, and
will be affirmed.

We proclaim the Good News that in Christ the walls of separation have been broken and that we are made One. We put our faith in the power of the Holy Spirit to redeem the structures of the Church so they will more faithfully reflect God's design for the liberation and wholeness of each human being and the world.

The Greek word for the timing of our actions is *kairos*, "God's time." *Kairos* cannot be calculated by clocks, calendars, or conventions. *Kairos* bursts without warning into *chronos*, "human time." Each time this happens—and it is always happening—the very human question is posed: "Why couldn't you wait?" "The change was coming." "The time was coming." "People were almost ready." *Kairos is always too soon.* We are never "ready" for it. But occasionally we will know that the time is at hand. We will know that we are ready. Trembling and laughing, we will choose to go forth.

Four days before the Riverside service, Victor Schramm, a priest from Michigan and the master of ceremonies for the upcoming service, joined me in a visit to Paul Moore's apartment. I had written to Paul about our intentions to participate in this celebration, but I wanted to discuss the matter with him in person.

The visit was a relaxed one. Paul listened intently as I explained to him why I believed we must take this step, and others after it, in order to be faithful to our vocations. He told me that, while he wished the service were not happening, he also wished he could be present with us. I invited him to come concelebrate with us. He laughed and said that he would be on vacation in Connecticut that evening. He indicated that he had no idea of what reactions we would reap, but that he would do everything he could to maintain peace in the diocese.

He told me I looked tired and to get some rest. I detected sadness in his voice and face. That night, after describing my visit with the bishop in a conversation with my apartment-mate,

Jean, I cried myself to sleep. Empathy? Tension? Tiredness? Alienation? Anger? A lingering need for my Father-in-God's approval? Maturation into new levels of faith and activity? A little of each.

> *Go to hell, buck teeth! Someone ought to kill you. You're filthy.*
> —Anonymous note, fall, 1974.

STATEMENT BY THE CELEBRANTS—

On July 29, 1974, four Episcopal bishops ordained eleven women deacons to the priesthood. On this occasion, the eleven of us agreed to refrain from exercising publicly our priestly functions for a time. Our hope was that the ecclesiastical authorities of our church would move quickly to regularize our ordinations and ordain our sister deacons to the priesthood.

However, on August 15, the House of Bishops expressed its conviction that our ordinations are invalid. At that time, we issued a statement that we could not accept the bishops' decision, and that each of us would decide when and how to affirm the priesthood into which she has been ordained.

By late September, we had become aware that the time had come for some of us to publicly proclaim the validity of the Philadelphia ordinations and, in so doing, the valid and critical ministry of all women.

Hence, in cooperation with women in ministry from various denominations, three of us began to plan towards a Service in Celebration of Women in Ministry. We three decided that, upon such an occasion, we would celebrate the Eucharist according to the Episcopal Church's Authorized Services, 1973. Women from other denominations, as well as our own, have been instrumental in the planning and implementation of such a service, believing, as we all do, that what has transpired in the Episcopal Church is not peculiarly an "Episcopal" problem. It is a problem facing the whole Christian Church: fundamental to church life, women remain peripheral, ignored, and invisible within its processes.

Therefore, on October 27—Reformation Sunday—the three of us join women and men throughout the church in witnessing to a common faith. Our faith is in a God who has heard our cries; who is building a community in which we find joy and grace; and who has strengthened us and called us forth to bear this witness. Such witness was made on July 29 by nearly 2000 people. On October 27, the witness continues.

On October 17, the House of Bishops reaffirmed its support of women's ordination, in principle. While we rejoice in this action, we must note that women do not exist merely "in principle." We are people and we are priests—not an hypothesis, but a reality. Our vocation does not lie dormant as a future possibility. The call, the time, is now.

We call upon Episcopal bishops and other ecclesiastical authorities to hear us, and to join us. Our Anglican tradition means much to us. In it we have our roots. We pray that it will be opened soon to embrace the dignity of all persons. Then, and only then, can Episcopalians stand together—in reconciliation and in true community—as ministers to a needy world.

In joy, knowing pain; in peace, acknowledging the conflict in which we participate, we celebrate this strange and wonderful movement of the Holy Spirit who brings us to this night. We recall especially the Spirit's movement among women throughout all times.

Finally, we offer this Eucharist to the Glory of Almighty God; and in thanksgiving for the ministry of our sister priests—Betty, Marie, Alla, Sue, Emily, Nancy, Katrina, Merrill; for the ministry of our sister deacons, especially Lee, who is being ordained tonight in Washington; for the ministry of our sisters among the laity; for the ministry of our brother bishops—especially Daniel, Robert, Antonio, Edward; and for the ministry of all women, and men who have stood with us, in all churches, in all ages.

—Alison Cheek, Carter Heyward, Jeannette Piccard

As we lifted the bread, baked by women from St. Stephen's in Washington, above our heads to break it in the offering of sacrifice, I recalled momentarily the flowers that had been sent to us prior to the service and the anonymous card that had accompanied them: *"Let the Spirit flow! Love, Melchizedek."*

For me it's like a great weight being gone. . . . Hooray!
—Letter to me from woman seminarian,
Church Divinity School of the Pacific,
Berkeley, California, summer, 1974.

Dear Bishop Allin [Presiding Bishop of the Episcopal Church]:

Last night was a splendid and Spirit-filled occasion for us and for many of our sister and brother Christians here in New York and elsewhere. Please find enclosed both a copy of the bulletin from the Celebration of Women in Ministry and a check for $672, collected during the Offertory and made payable to your Fund for World Relief. This comes in recognition of the gross human suffering in the world and in response to the Bishop of New York's diocesan-wide appeal for Episcopal commitment to "hunger relief."

Your sisters in Christ,

Alison Cheek, Carter Heyward, Jeannette Piccard

I pray this will bring a new day in the life of the church everywhere.

—Letter to me from United Methodist laywoman and seminary professor, New Jersey, fall, 1974.

TO THE CLERGY OF THE DIOCESE OF NEW YORK—

Dear Friends:

Last Sunday, the Rev. Carter Heyward, a deacon of our diocese who was ordained a priest irregularly (some, including the House of Bishops, say invalidly) in Philadelphia on July 29th celebrated the Eucharist at Riverside Church. Two similarly ordained clergy from other dioceses concelebrated with her....

No one of the three clergy is recognized as a priest of our Church. The service, therefore, was not in accord with the doctrine, discipline and worship of our Church. As Bishop I directed the Rev. Carter Heyward to refrain from exercising priesthood. She deliberately defied this directive and in so doing alienated herself from the regular life and discipline of this diocese....

I hereby formally reprimand the Rev. Carter Heyward for this action and inhibit the Rev. Alison Cheek of the Diocese of Virginia and the Rev. Jeannette Piccard of the Diocese of Minnesota from ministry in this diocese....

I do not use strong words lightly. I have been sympathetic and patient, seeking by persuasion and support of the cause to avoid this situation. However, the service of October 27th demands a response.

This action is contrary to a clear directive of the bishop, has upset the majority of clergy and laity of the diocese, has set back the mission of the Church in this place, and has jeopardized some delicate ecumenical relations.

I offer my heartfelt sympathy to those who are confused by these events. You need to be confused no longer. Neither this nor any similar acts are an acceptable part of the life of this diocese.

Even though I am sure this action was done in conscience, it is ironic that its consequences probably will set back the very cause for which these women have worked and for which I have worked over the past few years, namely the full acceptance of women as priests and bishops of the Church. It is also ironic that our mission to the desperate plight of this city and its environs may be set back by what seemed to the participants to be an act of liberation.

However, there is great spiritual power being raised up in our land and in our Church through the women's movement. The Lord will use this power for good. He will redeem us all and, even through this conflict, bring forth a mightier Church in which men and women, priests and lay persons, will minister together in the authority and power of His love.

> Sincerely,
> Paul Moore, Jr., Bishop of New York

At this time it is perhaps most important that your fellow priests who support you and the other female priests of the church make our feelings known.... I respect your courage to follow in the tradition of Luther, proclaiming "Here I stand, I can do no other."
> —Letter to me from priest,
> Diocese of New York, fall, 1974.

Dear Carter:

This is to acknowledge your letter of October 28th with the enclosed check in the amount of $672. It is with deep regret that I must return this check to you but I am compelled to do so as a matter of conscience. I have come to hope that you and your sisters may reach the proper goals of your vocations. I am sorry that at this point I cannot accept the means you have chosen. With good wishes for you,

> I am faithfully yours,
> John M. Allin, PRESIDING BISHOP

Thank you for removing the Ordination of Women to the Priest-hood from the realms of academic exercises to that of reality. The Church's first reaction was pure panic; in time she will settle down and bring Canon law up to date.
—Letter to me from Anglican priest,
Nova Scotia, Canada, fall, 1974.

Dear Paul:

Members of St. Mary's Church, its clergy, and a number of us who participated in the Riverside Service have agreed that the money should be sent to you—for the same purpose. Perhaps you will be able to convince Bishop Allin that the money is not "tainted." I have enclosed the check, now redrawn, and made payable to you in the sum of $672.

Sincerely,
Carter

Paul Moore took the money and sent it himself to the Presiding Bishop's Fund for World Relief. It was accepted.

Dear Paul:

You may have heard already that I plan to celebrate the Eucharist at Christ Church, Oberlin, on December 8. As with the Riverside service, this decision has not been made lightly. I both regret that things "have" to be this way and marvel at whatever is happening within so many people in our own church these days. There is Life! Please pray for me, and I will, and do, for you, Paul.

Sincerely,
Carter

I rejoice with you at this beginning of your public priestly minis-try! You have been for me and many others our priest long even before July 29.
—Letter to me from woman deacon,
Diocese of Southern Ohio, fall, 1974.

I tell you, you are Peter, and on this rock I will build my church, and the powers of death shall not prevail against it.
Matthew 16:18

When Jesus charged Peter to be the rock upon which the Church would be built, what do you suppose he had in mind for Peter: A cope and mitre? or an inverted cross?

Alison Cheek and I drove home together from Ohio on May 15, 1975. For three days, we had been participants in the ecclesiastical trial of Peter Beebe, rector of Christ Church, Oberlin, charged with disobeying the "godly admonition" of Bishop John H. Burt and with violating the Constitutions and Canons of the Church by allowing two "unauthorized ministers" to preside at the Eucharist in his parish.

We, the unauthorized ministers, spent our journey reflecting on the trial and all that had led up to it, specifically the spiritual community we had experienced among the Oberlin people, and the example of discipleship manifest by Peter Beebe.

Peter is young. His is a powerful spiritual presence. He is compelling enough a figure to have been chosen a cardinal rector, or elected a bishop, at an unusually young age were he to have played his cards right. Or perhaps Peter would never have "made it." Perhaps his charisma derives from his courage. Perhaps Peter has always been "ecclesiastically hopeless," a step beyond the normal cleric in his compulsion to do what is right. His name is fitting for, like his apostolic ancestor, Peter Beebe seems bent upon allegiance to Christ, at whatever the cost. Hence, neither he nor we could have been too surprised when the Ecclesiastical Court of the Diocese of Ohio ordered Peter to halt his "ministry of affirmation and compassion to persons suffering outrageously inequitable and humiliating treatment by the authorities of this Church," and instead to be obedient to these authorities. And the ecclesiastical authorities could not have been too surprised when Peter Beebe ignored this directive.

The church at Oberlin is a Good News church! It is full of the Spirit; conscious of its Christian call to spirituality, community, and justice; open to its own internal conflicts which cannot be swept under a carpet any more effectively than a cancer can be camouflaged under a Band-Aid.

Christ Church, Oberlin, has become a home for women priests

—a place in which we can be who we are, lifted by its spiritual buoyancy. The church at Oberlin joined the church of St. Stephen and the Incarnation in Washington, D.C., as one of the first Episcopal parishes to open its doors to the ministry of women priests.

What motivates a congregation to step beyond the boundaries of ecclesiastical authority and issue its own call to "unauthorized ministers"? To take the law into its own hands, as it were, and to live according to the mandates of a faith that the ecclesiastical authorities profess but do not act upon? I believe very much the same Spirit that drove hundreds of Episcopalians to Philadelphia.

My relationship to Oberlin began in September, 1974, two months after the ordination. Sue Hiatt had been invited to Christ Church to preach. By coincidence (if there is such a thing), I had been asked to appear on a television program in Cleveland the same weekend. Hence, both Sue and I wound up attending the Oberlin parish and leading a congregational forum on women's ordination in general, our own ordinations in particular.

At that time Peter told us that the Philadelphia ordinations, together with the House of Bishops' reaction to it, had awakened him not only to the plight of *women* in the Church, but moreover to the plight of *Christians* in the Church. The issue had become for him not simply that of "women's ordination," but also that of "authority": When push comes to shove, to whom or what are we ultimately accountable as Christian people?

Christ Church itself was in process of becoming a parish in which the priesthood of all believers is a functional reality rather than a doctrinal catch phrase. The two ordained ministers had been serving as functionaries (pastors, counselors, consultants) and sacramentalists. There seemed to be nothing hokey about this *modus operandi*. The church at Oberlin was not a parish in which a "with-it" priest could espouse shared leadership and simultaneously manipulate the congregation into believing it was making its own decisions. Nor is there a suspect "sweetness" in the Oberlin air. The parish life has had an authentic ring to it, perhaps partly because the human conflict, usually so well concealed from strangers in a parish, is so openly present, perturbing and painful to each person at Christ Church who feels anything at stake in the life of the parish.

In October, four members of the Oberlin Congregation, including Peter, had driven to New York to attend the Service in Celebration of Women in Ministry. Following the service, they had talked to some of us about the possibility of our coming to Oberlin later in the year to serve as priests on a Sunday morning and to further the pastoral relationship already begun between the parishioners and women priests. The women priests gathered in my apartment with the Oberlin folks on this occasion agreed that we as a group could support wholeheartedly such an endeavor and that at least two of us would be available to go to Oberlin on December 8, if officially invited to do so.

The parish was by no means unanimous in its invitation. But a significant majority among the congregation, supported by the rector and a 6–5 majority of the vestry, called us to come. Thus began an extraordinary relationship between two of us and an Episcopal parish.

> *We are eagerly looking foward to December 8th, and your celebrating in Oberlin. Plans are underway—Peter is wisely involving all of the parish in small discussion groups.... Thank God for such priests. It behooves all of us to work to keep men like him and women like you "eleven" in this Church so that it will be worth more than just an "organization."*
> —Letter to me from laywoman, Diocese of Ohio, fall, 1974.

Soon after my official invitation to celebrate at Christ Church, Oberlin, I received a long letter from Ohio Bishop John H. Burt, imploring me not to come. He felt that the celebration of the Eucharist by women celebrants would upset many members of the parish. Bishop Burt commented that, whereas he does not like to resort to the use of canon law in his dealings with clergy, he would indeed be forced to forbid us, canonically, to come as priests into his diocese if we refused to heed voluntarily his pastoral plea.

From the beginning of our relationship with Christ Church, Oberlin, Bishop Burt, considered a strong supporter of women's ordination *in principle*, has maintained that his refusal to grant Alison Cheek and me permission to minister as priests in his diocese has *nothing to do with our being female*, but rather concerns our lack of impeccable "credentials"—i.e., proof, beyond any doubt, that we are priests.

Even though I am Catholic and not Episcopalian, I am in favor of women as priests. I now have a six-month-old daughter. I'd be very upset if I thought she would be prevented from doing anything she wanted simply because she were female. What you are doing is going to help her someday. Thank you.
—Letter to me from Roman Catholic laywoman, winter, 1974.

In late November, Paul Moore wrote and asked that I come to see him to talk things over. I knew that he was concerned about my going to Oberlin. I phoned and made an appointment.

I want to tell you of my support and admiration. I totally agree with you and your call and I'm proud of your courageous conviction. Do continue "fighting the good fight." . . . The time will come when the prophet's voice will be heard.
—Letter to me from Roman Catholic woman religious, fall, 1974.

Dear Bishop Burt:
   That you and other bishops of our church whom I know (personally or by reputation) to be sensitive and courageous leaders can continue to uphold your present stand on our ordinations saddens me. . . . Would you have requested a member of the clergy not to preach a controversial sermon on racism in 1960 or not to participate in the March on Washington in 1963 out of your "concern for the distress of many fine parishioners"? . . .
                              Sincerely,
                              (The Rev.) Carter Heyward.
P.S. I have enclosed a cartoon . . .

Dear Ms. Heyward:

Last Sunday, I spent six hours in Oberlin holding extended dialogue with the Rev. Peter Beebe, the Vestry and members of the Christ Church congregation assembled in public meeting.... I am sorry to report that I found parochial opinion badly divided, even polarized.... In an earlier letter to you, I pleaded pastorally that you withdraw your acceptance of the invitation to celebrate the Eucharist in Oberlin.... With deep personal regret, I must hereby formally and officially "admonish and inhibit" you from any attempt to officiate as a priest in the Diocese of Ohio until such time as I receive evidence from your diocesan [bishop] which may lead me to revoke this decision.... I express my appreciation in advance for your cooperation with this request.

Ever faithfully yours,
John H. Burt, Bishop of Ohio.

On December 4 I met with Paul Moore. The meeting was difficult. He was angry, shocked at my reply to Bishop Burt's first "pastoral" letter to me asking me not to come as a priest to Oberlin. My response to Bishop Burt's letter had indeed been somewhat intemperate, by ecclesiastical standards, for not only had I written that I was saddened by the bishops' stand and insulted by their invocation of canon law to deal with an urgent matter of ethical import; but also I had accused Bishop Burt of being an "organizational" man as to be blinded to the reality of women being dealt injustice. Furthermore, Paul Moore was extremely upset about the cartoon I had sent Bishop Burt.

Moreover, he seemed distressed that I intended to go on to Oberlin. He made several comments about the havoc I was wreaking on the Church and he seemed to feel hurt and betrayed by me. I listened and then explained as best I could what was going on within and around me, why I had decided to go to Oberlin, and why I would be going other places as well.

After I spoke, Paul said that he was glad I had come, that he again understood what I was doing and why, and that he hoped I would keep him posted. "I feel better!" he commented as I left, "I don't know whether you do or not." I shrugged my shoulders, laughed, and indicated that I was glad that some communication had been restored.

I pray for you often and in concern for what you are bearing on behalf of us all.
—Letter to me from diocesan bishop,
Province III (Mid-Atlantic states), winter, 1974.

Dear Bishop Burt:

In faith, I cannot cooperate with your request. As I prepare to leave momentarily for Oberlin, I find myself grateful, and joyful at the Spirit among the community of people who have invited us to join them in celebration; at the same time, sad that I join them without your approval and amid some division within the parish itself.

Sincerely,
(The Rev.) Carter Heyward

Dear Carter:

I am glad we met.... I still find us very far apart; this does distress and concern me, not just because of our relationship, but because of the good of the Church. In spite of this, I *was glad* to see you and do feel it is important for us to continue this communication. The reason for the enclosed letter was a request from Bishop Burt that I go on paper in this regard even though the substance is already included in previous communications between you and me.

Sincerely,
Paul, Bishop of New York.

Enclosure: Dear Carter: Just for the record, I wanted to put on paper my admonishing you not to celebrate the Eucharist at Oberlin.

Sincerely,
Paul Moore, Jr., Bishop of New York

Alison and I arrived in Oberlin on Friday night, December 6, 1974. For the next two days, we attended potlucks, parties, and meetings during which we had the opportunity to discuss the meaning of our presence with both proponents and opponents of our ordination and our "defiance." The associate rector told us he could not support our proposed action; elderly women in hospitals and nursing homes were elated that we were there. One vestryperson said that he could not defy his bishop; another commented that he could not, in this case, obey his bishop. Young women in the parish were manifestly moved by what our presence symbolized to them about themselves. Other women assured us that their support of us was, in large part, their affirmation of who they are, as full people of God. Men talked to us about their struggles to break out of gender-defined bondage.

Pro or con, each person who met with us seemed to have some sense of what Sunday's service might mean for the congregation in terms of ecclesiastical repercussion. People seemed to realize that the action could someday result in an actual split within the parish, for which few would wish but which most seemed willing to entertain as possibility if standing one's ground were to lead through trial courts in such a direction.

TO MEMBERS OF CHRIST CHURCH, OBERLIN—

Dear Friends:

We rejoice in your courage and witness as our sisters preside at your weekly Eucharists today. Another chapter has been added to Oberlin's long history of making "no peace with oppression." We are surprised to learn that we have been represented [by Bishop Burt] as divided in our support of you and of our sister priests. We affirm and respect each others' judgment as to how and when our priesthood will be exercised. We thank God for you, and for our sisters, Alison and Carter. We are with you in Spirit and in prayer.

Shalom! Merrill Bittner, Alla Bozarth-Campbell, Emily Hewitt, Suzanne Hiatt, Marie Moorefield, Jeannette Piccard, Betty Schiess, Katrina Swanson, Nancy Wittig.

During our weekend in Oberlin, Alison and I were filled with a sense of our membership and ministry within the Christ Church community. By Sunday morning, we knew that the December 8 celebration would be more a beginning than an end. We flew back East knowing that we would return as soon as possible.

> *The idea of the priesthood's being an exclusive men's club has gone. And if, in some of us, the emotional ties of this fad linger on, it has to be extirpated, especially as the consequences of our feeling are so hurtful to others . . . God grant you and your women colleagues peace and strength.*
>
> —Letter to me from layman,
> Diocese of New York, fall, 1974.

Dear Paul:

So that you will know—I will be presiding at a Eucharist at the United Nations this Sunday, December 15.

> Sincerely,
> Carter

> *Just a wee word to tell you I remember you, and your cause, every day in my Mass.*
>
> —Letter to me from Roman Catholic priest and monk,
> winter, 1974.

Dear Paul:

This coming weekend, Feb. 1–2, I am participating in a symposium on "Women and the Church" in Edinboro, Pa. The culmination of this event is to be a liturgy at which I have agreed to serve as celebrant. . . .

> Sincerely,
> Carter

> *When you, a female, spoke the words, "You are the source of light and life. You made us in your image," I felt taller. For the first time in my life, I felt included, as if I, too, am made in God's image. . . . Thank you.*
>
> —Letter to me from a woman religious,
> Diocese of New York, fall, 1974.

To: The Bishops of the Church and Alumni/ae and Friends of the Episcopal Divinity School.

From: Harvey H. Guthrie, Jr., and Edward G. Harris, Deans.

The Rev. Carter Heyward and the Rev. Suzanne Hiatt have been invited to become members of the faculty of our school with the usual rights, privileges and responsibilities that accompany faculty membership. . . .

Dear Paul:
[Regarding our earlier talk by phone], I have decided to accept the appointment to Episcopal Divinity School, beginning July 1, 1975. . . .

Sincerely,
Carter

All my life I have belonged to and loved the Episcopal Church. I still do and will pray for it. Now it is being undermined by Women's Lib (so-called). They call themselves Christians! And some, Episcopalians!

—Letter to me from laywoman,
Diocese of Nebraska, winter, 1975.

TO THE BISHOP AND STANDING COMMITTEE
OF THE DIOCESE OF NEW YORK—

Dear Bishop Moore and Ladies and Gentlemen of the Standing Committee:
. . . St. Mary's is the home church for Emily Hewitt and Carter Heyward, both ordained as priests at Philadelphia this past July. St. Mary's is the only Episcopal Church in the country which had two women deacons; and both are now priests. . . . The time is now, not at the next national convention. Your integrity and ours, and the integrity of the Episcopal Church, requires that we respond to this issue now—and not try to contain it. You, Bishop Moore, and you, members of the Standing Committee, can now issue a resolution confirming your conclusion that the Philadelphia ordinations were valid, whether or not irregular, and that the ordained women are authorized to act as priests in this diocese. . . . You can exert leadership. You can help the Episcopal Church to be vigorous and alive, and we desire to help you in this vigorous leadership. We do not want to receive from you a letter of sympathy for

the movement, or a hope that perhaps some time in the future this wrong can be righted....

Sincerely yours, the Rector, Rector Pro-Tem, Wardens and Vestry of St. Mary's Episcopal Church in Manhattanville, on behalf of the Congregation.

When you're through with these broads, don't send them to me.
     —Comment by a diocesan bishop, Province IV (South), to people of his diocese who were having a dicussion with several Episcopal women clergy.

Dear People of St. Mary's:

Receiving a letter like yours is frustrating, to say the least. I have, to the best of my ability, set forward the cause of women's ordination. I daresay that with the exception of the ordained women and candidates, I have spent more time and energy on this than anyone in this diocese. I am glad to do so.... The one thing I have not done is what I cannot do—regularize the orders on a Diocesan level.... In all sincerity, I must clearly say no. Any such action would bring more confusion and resentment and *would not* in fact regularize anything. If you wish to discuss the matter, I would be glad to see you. May I add that your letter brings *me* great anguish. I do not understand why you cannot comprehend my position.

Sincerely,
Paul Moore, Jr., Bishop of New York

Being with you puts me in touch with the priest in me.
     —Comment to me by woman seminarian, Union Theological Seminary, summer, 1975.

In February, 1975, the women priests met in Alexandria, Virginia. As we shared our experiences, we detected a common thread weaving among us: Our bishops were increasingly unable to relate to us pastorally. Somewhere along the way, the tables had turned, or so it seemed to us. We were finding ourselves in the role of being pastors to our bishops, of being asked to explain "the meaning of it all" to them every week or so. And we were not being very good pastors at that. For we were setting ourselves up before them only to get shot down, thereby making them "feel better," and simultaneously taking onto ourselves a slow, grueling psychic punishment without benefit of trial by the ecclesiastical authorities and structures of the Church.

We agreed that we needed to terminate this "pastoral process" —for our own sake, as well as for the sake of our bishops and the Church at large. We could no longer present ourselves irresponsibly as "whipping girls" for people in the Church, including our own bishops, whatever affection we felt for them.

Furthermore, we had become increasingly convinced that canon law is on our side—i.e., that we had been denied the due process to which every deacon, priest, and bishop of the Church is entitled. In attempting either to father us, or to protect their own professional interests, our bishops had failed to grant us the mature human dignity of even the ecclesiastical trial procedures, in which the validity of our ordinations might have been upheld, or if not that, at least our predicament acknowledged and dealt with openly and publicly.

Soon after, I met with my lawyer, Frank Patton, an Episcopal layman and member of St. Mary's Church. He had read all correspondence between Paul Moore and me, dating from long before the ordination. He listened to me relate my feelings and my ecclesiastical objectives as I anticipated the coming months—in New York, Cambridge, Oberlin. I said that I intended to be about my priestly ministry however and wherever I could, and that I hoped to be able to see my own and my sisters' orders "regularized" in as clean and clear a way as possible.

It was becoming clear to me that the "pastoral" relationship out of which Paul and I had been operating was, at best, inadequately pastoral and, at worst, an impediment to whatever legal proceedings might have to be undertaken someday to insure my participation in a "regularized" (i.e., normal) priesthood.

We say that the Holy Spirit is leading us.
They say that we should be more politically astute.

We say that this is a matter of vocational, professional, ethical and political imperative.

They say that we don't have enough faith in the Holy Spirit.

Dear Paul:

   My attorney, Frank Patton, and I have discussed my ecclesiastical situation at some length. He and I are in agreement that my ecclesiastical standing and my priestly activities are not a matter of pastoral relations, but rather constitute a serious legal matter. Therefore, upon his counsel, I have made some decisions: (1) To request that any correspondence you would send me regarding my priesthood be sent to my attorney.... (2) To tell you that I will no longer report to you the specificities of my public ministry; but rather, that I, like any member of the clergy, will submit to you an annual report of my ministerial functions (Title I, Canon 5, Section 1, "Of the Mode of Securing an Accurate View of the State of the Church").

                                                      Sincerely,
                                                      Carter

Paul responded with a question: What is going on?

I wanted to try to tell Paul what was "going on," to make one last attempt at communication before the entry into necessary silence between us. At last, I had to admit to myself that my relationship to my own bishop must be held at a distance—as a strictly professional and, for the time being, a legal matter.

Dear Paul:

   ...I cannot live in such *extraordinary duplicity*.... I cannot continue to affirm you as Paul Moore while I battle with you as the Bishop of New York; and I cannot believe myself affirmed by you as Carter Heyward, "a deacon of this diocese," and at the same time rejected by you as "a priest of the Church." My personhood, baptism, diaconate, priesthood, teaching, counseling, speaking and preaching engagements, celebrations of Eucharist, other activities, relationships, loves and hates are all bound up together in who I am. Carter Heyward the person *is* Carter Heyward the priest.... You will do what you believe you must and I'll do the same. By the grace and mystery of God, a healing of wounds may happen further down the road.

Sincerely,
Carter

For shame, that one who names herself a Christian should allow herself to cause such strife in Christ's Body, The Church. Why not withdraw and let there be peace. I shall pray for you.
—Letter to me from priest,
Diocese of Milwaukee, spring, 1975.

At the invitation of rector and vestry, Alison returned to Oberlin on Passion Sunday, 1975. Two weeks later, I joined the people of Christ Church for their Easter celebration. My friend, Eileen Jones, a body movement teacher in New York, accompanied me on this trip and was asked by a group of parishioners to lead a class in movement for them while Peter and I took Easter Communion to an infirm communicant on Saturday afternoon. Throughout the weekend, Eileen and I were hosted from feast to feast, service to service, and finally to an exceptional Easter banquet and egg hunt at the home of one of the parish families.

Offhandedly, I had mentioned to some of the children and young people that I loved Easter egg hunts and was disappointed that their hunt was to be only for those under eighteen. When we arrived for the banquet, Eileen and I were greeted by two of the girls, Mary McGill and Katie Nord, who themselves were flanked by expectant children. We were informed that a special egg hunt had been planned for us, and we were led, with care, from egg to egg on the basis of clever clues that Katie and Mary had devised. The final clue sent us scurrying into the yard with children galloping after us to watch us discover the treasures they had prepared: two Easter baskets full of white chocolate rabbits, jelly beans, and brilliantly color-swirled eggs.

As my Easter basket toppled through the screening device in Cleveland's Hopkins Airport, several parishioners joined me in flying leaps for eggs. I carried my gift home to New York every bit as tenderly as I did my stole and Bible.

> *Thank you for becoming a priest. I don't want to be a priest; I just want a woman who is a priest so that I may go to her.*
> —Letter to me from Roman Catholic laywoman, winter, 1975.

Charges had been brought against Peter for the December 8 service and his trial date set for mid-May, 1975. Alison and I had been notified by Peter's lawyer, John Rea, that we were to testify for the defense since the court had agreed to hear the question of our ordinations' validity. On Saturday, May 10, Eileen and I pulled into Oberlin—she, to do body work with the parishioners for fun and therapy; I, to participate in the weekly liturgy and to help prepare for trial.

As at Easter, we stayed with Cindy and Evan Nord, four of their children, and their three golden retrievers, in a spacious setting just right for meditation as well as camaraderie. On Sunday, May 11, Peter and Judy Beebe joined us for dinner in the backyard.

Soon in the evening, Peter and I decided to take a walk and talk. We rambled down to a nearby reservoir and sat down on its bank. We discussed the Church, and ourselves; the ways in which our lives had been altered over recent months; the integrity each of us had found in standing where she, or he, must; the fabulous authenticity of life in community we had experienced among people in Christ Church and elsewhere. We shared sadness in the alienation we had come upon in relationship to people to whom we had once been close. We shared questions about whether or not either of us could ever really be "acceptable" priests in the Episcopal Church, and about whether or not we would want to be, if it meant making the sorts of soulful compromises we had been asked to make so often these last months.

We talked about the upcoming trial and the need we felt to celebrate Holy Communion each day of the proceedings, and to speak repeatedly, and publicly, of the Gospel rather than allowing ourselves to be dragged into debating canon law for the sake

Banned from liturgical functioning in the church building, Episcopal priests Carter Heyward, Alison Cheek, and Peter Beebe leave ecclesiastical trial proceedings during noon recess to celebrate communion in a nearby park. Akron, Ohio, May 14, 1975.

of canon law. We confessed our guilt—our having hurt some people, our incapacities to hear some people, the risks we had taken. Perhaps we had been wrong? Perhaps we were being destructive to something good? We recalled conversations he and I had participated in with Bishops John Burt and Paul Moore, respectively, and with others who "could not" support what we were doing. We expressed regrets, confidence, misgivings, feelings of peace, and feelings of despondency that would occasionally creep into our psyches and pull us down.

We pulled ourselves up and headed back to the Nords. Within and between us, there was sadness, and satisfaction. We had chosen this way. If given the chance, we would do so again, with God's help.

On Monday, May 12, the night before the trial began in Akron, five women priests and five men priests concelebrated in Christ Church, Oberlin. I will long remember this service as *Holy Communion*. Peter's friend, Louis Gilbert, a Congregational minister and communicant of Christ Church, preached. And there together, male and female, priests flowed in and out from altar to communicants, rotating, exchanging paten (bread plate) for chalice, stepping back and resting, taking turns deaconing, and finally feeding each other.

> *Some people were arguing about whether or not so much time and energy should be spent on "women priests" when we need to be concerned about feeding people. An old woman spoke up, "What the hell do you think this is all about?"*
> —Priest, Diocese of Washington, spring, 1975.

After the service, as I shed my vestments in the Oberlin sacristy, a young girl, Fifi, came up to me:

"Reverend Heyward, will you do something for me? Will you wear this ring?"

I glanced at the narrow hand-crafted silver band she held out. I smiled and nodded, reached for it and slipped it on the middle finger of my right hand. "My goodness, Fifi, thank you!"

"Oh, Reverend Heyward, thank you for what you and the others are doing for us!" She flung her arms around me in a tearful embrace.

For all my low church tendencies, and despite my renunciation of my Catholic traditions, being a witness to the events surrounding your ordination has been a smashing, powerful experience for me.
—Letter to me from United Church of Christ clergywoman, Chicago, winter, 1975.

FROM THE COMMENT OF THE ECCLESIASTICAL COURT OF THE
DIOCESE OF OHIO

The Standing Committee of The Diocese of Ohio
v.
The Reverend L. Peter Beebe

... The first condition of which we take note is the essentially unjust, inequitable and unfair way in which the Ordination (and therefore the licensing) canons of this Church are at present administered by Bishops and Standing Committees. We refer, of course, to the fundamentally inequitable, discriminatory and systematic exclusion of well trained, well qualified and godly persons from the Order of Priests in this Church solely, exclusively and specifically because such persons are women. We have heard, through testimony and evidence, that the principals in the service of December 8th at Christ Church, Oberlin, Ohio, were in all respects qualified to serve as priests of the Church, the sole reason for their rejection by their Bishops and Standing Committees being that they are women. We believe that this notorious inequity gravely affects and taints the entire system of canon law as pertaining to ordination and licensing. Having been denied, through this inequitable system, their legitimate aspirations and vocations, the two women involved sought and received Ordination to the Priesthood by irregular means. That persons should seek justice through irregular means when the regular means are corrupted by inequitable and discriminatory elements is both reasonable and fundamentally fair. That they should be required to do so by a Christian Church is a scandal not only to the faithful but also to all reasonable and fair people everywhere.

Mr. Beebe, in response to these women and their predicament, took upon himself the responsibility of affording them an opportunity to exercise a ministry elsewhere denied them. In so doing, he broke the law, a law which under normal and usual circumstances is both fair and necessary for the good ordering of the Church. We have found him guilty as charged on that count, but we must take notice, with deepest regret, that in the circumstances of his disobedience we find a sincere endeavor to extend a ministry of affirmation and compassion to persons suffering outrageously inequitable and humiliating treatment by the authorities of this Church. . . .

RECOMMENDATIONS

We unanimously recommend to the Bishop of Ohio, . . . that he admonish The Reverend L. Peter Beebe to refrain from any further violation of Title III.24 of the Canon Law of the Episcopal Church until the last day of the General Convention of this Church to be assembled in 1976. On that day such admonition shall be lifted in the event that the General Convention shall have failed to amend the ordination and licensing canons of this Church in such a way as to remove the inequitable, discriminatory and unfair practices which now abide in this Church. Furthermore, we unanimously and regretfully recommend, that if The Rev. L. Peter Beebe fails to comply with this further admonition he be suspended from the exercise of his ordained ministry until such time as he shall certify in writing to the Bishop, his willingness to comply.

Signed this Twentieth day of June in the year of our Lord, Nineteen Hundred Seventy-Five at Cleveland, Ohio.

> James D. Reasner, Judge and President of the Court;
> Ora A. Calhoun, Judge;
> Richard M. Morris, Judge;
> George E. Ross, Judge;
> George H. Van Doren, Judge.

The ecclesiastical trial was as peculiar, and terrifying, as the contradiction between the court's opinion and its recommendation. Picture the sanctuary and the long windows protecting the nave from all unholiness that lurks without. There is a narrow, white-draped table at the top of the chancel stairs and, behind it, five male judges robed in black and framed by pulpit, lectern, and the cross of Jesus. There is a thickness in the air, a sensation in the stomach, a feel about the place that there is here present some organic malevolence. You have entered a place in which the gavel and the Lord's Prayer will run concurrently along the same track—and where, if the spirit of one must get bumped off, it will be the latter. The Ecclesiastical Trial 1975, in which human integrity and Christian conscience will be put to the test; in which a bishop of the Church will be exempt from swearing to tell the truth and will state his conviction that a priest must obey his bishop even if the bishop is wrong; in which the judges will imply that the defendant acted according to the will of God and in which the same judges will hold that Peter Beebe must be restrained from such behavior. If you did not know better, you would think you had been spun back through a time zone and were observing the procedures of a Spanish Inquisition.

But you know better, and you do the only things you can. You worship with your community of friends and strangers. You sing. You hold on. You consult with William Stringfellow and plan with John Rea, defense lawyer. From time to time you wink at Peter and Judy Beebe. And sooner or later, you cry, because it hurts.

Alison wept in Akron. She is a person whose feelings are so keenly integral to her being that she will not for long deny herself this reality. A day and a half later, upon our return from the trial, Alison and I sank into my living room chairs and attempted to assure each other that we were, in fact, still alive and in some touch with the real world.

I found myself speechless. I began to cry, and Alison conforted me, encouraging me to go ahead and empty myself of the emotional poison I had been fed in Akron.

I want to assure you of my prayers during what must be a difficult and frustrating time.
—Letter to me from priest, Diocese of East Carolina, fall, 1974.

Yes, trembling and laughing, vulnerable and strong, poisoned and made well, we go on, believing that our ordination was not an anomalous confrontation which, like an unusual craft, can be displayed on an ecclesiastical shelf as a curiosity piece; a trophy from battle; a token of experience; or an object of study, admiration, or regret. The ordination was not simply an "event" in the life of the Church. It was part of a *process*, which neither began nor ended in Philadelphia. A process in which *kairos* bursts—intrudes—into the order of things. A process in which the Spirit moves, renewing the church. In it, and with it, and by its holy power, we are graced to move with this God to court, celebration, and peace.[14]

And, I must say as we go, that I cannot fully understand the nature or the power of the symbol we embody as we go. Something extraordinary is happening. God is happening.

> *I did not expect to be so personally affected by your presence here. I was unaware of the ways that I have felt excluded from God's inner circle of love until I experienced being included—both by the obvious fact of your inclusion and by you, as God's representative, including me. Somehow I feel I've spent my life trying to be God's son, only to realize at last that I am God's daughter.*
> —Letter to me from laywoman, Diocese of Atlanta, winter, 1975.

An Easter Sermon[15]

Then Pilate said to him, "Do you not hear how many things they testify against you?" But he gave him no answer, not even to a single charge; so that the governor wondered greatly.

> Matthew 27:13–14

Pilate was a good man. A conscientious person. A leader of the people: responsible to the people, accountable to the people, protector of the people, open to the wishes and persuasions of the people, not one to force his will upon the people at the expense of their own.

It is often easy to identify with the protagonists of the stories we read, or see on TV or at the movies. It is much more difficult, I find, to enter into the characters of the antagonists of these stories.

We Christians not only take some comfort in seeing ourselves as the twentieth-century "Jesuses" of the Passion Story, but we are *encouraged* moreover to identify ourselves with Christ. If not to imitate him, then at least to so closely follow him that we do indeed grow more and more into a perception of ourselves— individually and collectively—as miniature models, however imperfect, of One who loved God and neighbor, who died for this love, and who rose again to perpetuate the power of this love.

Whether or not we know exactly what we mean, we call ourselves "disciples," those who have invested something in "being like the Master." We see ourselves as the contemporary manifestation of the Master, "the Body of Christ." We are Christians. We are the Church. And all around us, indeed within us (if we are psychologically astute), we locate and encounter, with chagrin, the "Pilates" and the "Judases" in our lives.

We disdain Pilate's weakness, his inability to say "no" to the roaring crowds and the duplicity with which he washed his hands of Christ's blood. We are mortified by the insidious and hideous betrayal done to Jesus by his self-seeking, sinister friend, Judas Iscariot. We, who are Christ, we who are the Church, find ourselves spending a significant part of our lives fending off Judas and Pilate—whether through therapy, protests and marches, self-discipline, boycotts, prayer, letter-writing campaigns, punishment, law-making, law-breaking, or perhaps most commonly, by simply sealing ourselves off in one way or another from those things or ideas or people whom we believe to be "bad," or destructive to what is "good."

And so, most of us live our lives in closets: warm and holy places, self-protected from evil and selfish impulses (hear no evil, see no evil, speak no evil, do no evil). Self-defended from the wrong kinds of people (Don't fall in with the wrong crowd. Don't follow the crowd). And self-closed to wrong thinking, wrong behavior, wrong worldview, wrong religion, bad faith. The Ten Commandments, Baptismal vows, Confirmation vows, Marriage vows, Ordination vows. Vows. Promises. Pledges. And prizes for right thinking and good behavior.

In order to play Christ, we must be careful. In order to be Christian, we must be good, or at least try to be good. In order to *be* at all, we must *beware*, lest we be either the bearer or the recipient of some hurt or cruel distress to someone, perhaps even ourselves.

But I have a thesis and it is this: *That until we not only see ourselves, but strongly and gently embrace ourselves, as the Judas and the Pilate of the Passion Story, we cannot be the Christ of this story.* We cannot be who we are called to be as Christian people. We can pretend, and we can do all manner and means of things that are good and helpful to many. We can worship. We can work hard. We can teach. We can pray. We can visit the sick and minister to the poor and the dying. We can care for children. We can respect parents. We can send money and food to the hungry until all the hungry are fed. We can obey bishops. We can disobey bishops. We can discipline priests. We can be priests—whether we are women or men. But, until we are able to look at ourselves as in a mirror and see reflected there not only Jesus of Nazareth hanging on a cross, but also Judas Iscariot kissing his cheek, and Pontius Pilate turning his back and washing his hands, until we can know ourselves—and celebrate ourselves—as Judas and Pilate, we cannot be the Body of Jesus Christ. We cannot be the Church.

And so I ask you to enter with me, imaginatively, into the character of Pilate; and to see me, if you can, and yourselves, if you choose, as Pontius Pilate:

"My name is Pilate. Writing this book. Standing in a pulpit, sitting in my office, my kitchen, the classroom, I am wondering what it's all about. I have for some time now realized the awesomeness of my responsibilities.

"I, Pilate, am a priest of the church, and not just any priest, mind you: I am *a woman priest*. Responsible to the people of the church who, like myself, are deeply concerned about the state of affairs in the church, and in the world. People who, like myself, are in deep ways alienated from the church. I am responsible to

these people. That's inherent in my ordination vows: called forth
by God from within the community, to be a priest among the
people. I cannot go it alone. I cannot do it alone. I am one of
the people, responsible first and foremost to these people—in
Oberlin, Reading, New York, Cambridge, North Carolina,
Texas, Georgia, California. I feel the weight of the people. I feel
your weight. And I carry it, just as I am carried and supported
by the people. By *you*.

"I, Pilate, am also a teacher: responsible to my students and
my other colleagues at the seminary. I, Pilate, am also a friend,
and a sister, and a daughter: responsible to friends, sisters and
brothers, parents and family. You and I may be other things as
well, if not in fact, in possibility: a spouse, a mother, a father, a
businessperson, a school child, student, a person accountable to
other people. Living not simply according to our own wills, but
according to the needs, requests, dictates, sometimes even demands, of those to whom we are responsible.

"My name is Pilate: Leader. Teacher. Priest. Parent. Child.
Adult. Businessperson. Bishop. I try to do what is best for all
concerned. I try to do it honestly, wisely, with compassion and
integrity. *I am a responsible person.*

"And so it was that on that strange day, they brought to me
Jesus, who they said claimed to be 'King of the Jews,' or to put it
another way, they brought to me this person who, they said,
posed a serious threat to my authority, my well-being, my life-
style, a threat to everything that mattered to me, including the
welfare of my family and friends, and including my own vocation.

"They asked me to do something with this person, to put him
away, to screw him to the wall, nail him to the cross, crucify
him. They were afraid, and so was I, I must confess, partly
because *they* were, and they were *my people*, to whom I was
responsible. I had never seen them so badly agitated. And although I could not understand just why this particular person
scared them so—for he had done nothing particularly frightful
that I could see—I began to feel afraid myself. Fear is contagious.

"Fearfully, I reflected: Ah yes! Barabbas. I offered them Barabbas, clearly a criminal so frightful as to be unthinkable for them. I could release one prisoner this feast day, and I knew they'd rather have this strange Jesus back among them than Barabbas.

"I was wrong.

" 'Give us Barabbas!' they cried.

"This further frightened me. I could not imagine what Jesus had said or done, or could do, that would be so fearful to the people, anymore than I can imagine a baby dachshund posing a threat to a great dane or a VW to a Mack Truck. But the fear was apparent. And I felt myself break into a cold sweat.

"I had pleaded with Jesus to say something, to explain himself, to tell his side of this extraordinary situation. But he had only stood there silently, looking at me as if he had nothing to say. Only silence to contribute to the chaos. And that made me mad. But not being a person who wants her feelings to get the best of her, I swallowed my anger and continued to reflect.

"Getting no help from Jesus, I turned again to the people:

" 'What has he done?' I pled again with them. But this seemed only to exacerbate an already unbearable dilemma.

"Getting no help from the people, I turned back to Jesus. I looked at him. I flinched. I squinted. And I closed my eyes. To my great wonder, faces began to appear before me. I saw each and then went on to the next, or rather perhaps, each next one seemed to come on to me: my parents, my brother and sister, my playmates, my friends, my lovers, my students, my teachers, my bishops, my parishioners, my colleagues, indeed myself: *Each one victimized at some point in time or space by my fear of losing my own authority. Each, wounded by my insecurity.*

"No angrier at Jesus Christ than at the Bishop of New York; no angrier at this One Jesus, than at each of these people I have perceived as a threat to my own being; no angrier at any of these, than at myself, I opened my eyes and glared at Jesus.

"A silent moment passed, and I asked for some water. I washed my hands, and I spat out my judgment. 'I am innocent. You are guilty,' I nodded to the people. *Abdicating all authority for this death, forgetting that it was precisely in order to protect my authority that I was doing this,* I chose to blame Jesus' death on mass psychology, the corporate psychosis of the world, the church, our social institutions.

"And so, Jesus was beaten and mocked and led away to be crucified.

"My name is Pilate. I am a priest of the Church. I am a seminary teacher. I am a person, very much like any other person. I am afraid of my irresponsibility. I fear that my inadequacies will wind up crucifying people against whom I have nothing really. I am afraid that I will be a bad priest. A selfish friend. A poor mother or father. A destructive lover. A weak student. An irrelevant teacher. A basically weak-kneed woman who only pretends to be calm, cool, collected, courageous. I am afraid that I may turn my back on others at any moment. I cannot bear the guilt and the burden of responsibility, for I now see myself as irresponsible. My name is Pilate, and I am ashamed of what I did to Jesus three days ago.

"Lying in my bed, I begin to wake restlessly. It's early. I'm depressed—and still tired. Sleeping it off has made me only sleepier. But being the governor of the province, being a priest of the Church, being a person with work to do, classes to meet, meetings to hold, I pull myself up by my own bootstraps (as I have been taught), and I rise.

"Into the kitchen. Put on the coffee. Into the bathroom. Start the tub. Into the hall. Pick up the newspaper. Into the world. Sigh.

"It is early on the third day. Jesus is dead and buried. And I am alive and buried. And hurried. And hassled. I wish it hadn't happened. But it did. I wish I could forget. But I can't. Guilt put me to sleep. Perhaps guilt will allow me to continue sleeping as I move through this day.

"I take my bath and eat my breakfast. I read the *New York Times*, only to see of course that burial services have been held for Jesus Jones and Jesus Rodriguez and Jesus Smith, and that Jesus so-and-so was bombed in Cambodia and Ireland, and that Jesus is starving to death in Bangladesh and Appalachia, and that Jesus Gose has been admonished by Jesus Gressle and Jesus Beebe is being tried by Jesus Burt. I wash my hands, and I go into the bedroom to get dressed.

"Reaching into the top drawer for my clerical collar, I glance forward a little into the mirror. It's the first time in a long time I've looked at myself. I move a little closer, and engage myself with my eyes:

"I am full of wonder! For there in front of me I do not see a hardened destructive governor. I do not see a hard, tough woman priest. I do not see the perfect mother, father, or child. I do not see a shrewd businessperson. I do not see a brilliant student or teacher. I do not see an invulnerable lover. I do not see a tough-minded, unbending bishop.

"I see a human being, with soft sad eyes. I see tears. I see tiredness and pain and guilt. Looking even more deeply into those eyes, I see what is invisible to the eye: I see hope, and dreams, and longing, and intentions, and caring, and talent, and deep deep depth. I feel my hands. They are warm and moist, and maybe even bloody. I sense my breathing. It is full and heavy and rich, broken only by a gasp for deeper breath. I widen my eyes, and a few tears drop from my well, and through them I see glistening in the water and in the eyes themselves. I see light. I am becoming awakened to something good. I am beginning to feel alive!

"Breathing deeply, I close my eyes. And again, a stream of faces rolls before me: parents, sisters, brothers, friends and lovers, bishops, other colleagues, students and teachers, indeed myself again. Each of us, and all of us, alone and together alone, partners and soulmates in community with humankind. Each of us, and all of us, perhaps stretched with open arms onto a cross. Letting myself sink and rise in realization of our terrible oneness as sisters and brothers, letting myself drift and soar in acknowledgment of our simple and shared humanness, I open my eyes to see.

"I see the daylight breaking in the mirror. I am beginning to feel like myself again, no less the weak and wobbly person who sent Jesus to the cross, and no less a caring, human, person myself. No less guilty, I am beginning to experience grace. No less Pilate, the governor, I am beginning to wonder if perhaps my being is rooted in all human beings, including each person I have sent to death. No less an accuser, I am beginning to see myself as accused, screwed to the wall, nailed to the cross. No less a sinner, I am beginning to feel peace within myself.

"Extending myself forward, I look and I think that I see his own silent eyes in that mirror. His own scarred and bloody head as my own. I reach out for this reflection, to touch it, drawn by it. I reach out to touch myself. To shake hands with myself. To embrace myself. And in the distance, a voice—maybe it's the centurion, or maybe it's one of the women—seems to be shouting:

" 'HE IS RISEN!' "
Amen!

SHE IS RISEN!
Alleluia!

Commenting upon The Canterbury Statement's[17] assessment of the ordained priesthood, J. Robert Wright calls our attention to a piece of the backdrop of the Statement.[18] He notes that a Dominican scholar, commissioned by The Anglican-Roman Catholic International Commission, suggests that there are at least *five* "sorts" of "priesthood" that must be considered in the formulation of any doctrine on the nature of the ordained priesthood. One is the Old Testament's Levitical priesthood. The second is the priesthood of Christ, about which the book of Hebrews speaks most explicitly. The third is the priesthood of the Church (which I have called the priesthood of all believers). The fourth is the ordained ministry: a presbyterate-priesthood, comprised originally of "elders" appointed by the early Church for what seem to have been functional leadership roles. And the fifth is also the ordained priesthood, conceptualized as something of a "blending" of the second and the fourth sorts of priesthood: the priesthood of Christ and the priesthood of the presbyter/elder. Wright notes that the first three types of priesthood—Levitical, Christ's priesthood, and the priesthood of the church—all derive their meaning from the same Greek work: *hiereus*, which in Hebrew translates *kohen.* The word means "priest" and in all three contexts implies a "holiness of life" and a sacrificial function, although in each of the three cases the sacrificial offering is of a different sort.

The fourth type of priesthood—that of ordained people— is different from the first three. The Canterbury Statement reads: "[Ordained priesthood] is not an extension of the common Christian priesthood but belongs to another realm of the gifts of the Spirit." Wright suggests that this distinction is rooted in an early hermeneutic: Whereas the first three sorts of priesthood derive from the Greek and Hebrew words meaning "priest," the fourth sort of priesthood derives from the Greek word *presbyteros*, meaning "elder." The implication here is that the earliest leaders of the Christian community, commissioned by the "priesthood of the Church" for functional roles, were neither called nor considered "priests," but rather were commissioned to hold offices within the Church as "elders," presumably involved in "another realm of the gifts of the Spirit."

Yet, by the time of the Church Fathers—writing in the first several centuries A.D.—both *presbyteroi*/elders and *episcopoi*/"overseers" had begun to take on connotations from the first three sorts of priesthood: added to their functional roles within the community were the qualities of "holiness" and "sacrifice." It was from this linguistic, functional, and ontological merger that the fifth mode of priesthood apparently developed—that within which the *presbyteros/hiereus, or elder/priest, is seen as not only functionally distinct from the priesthood of all believers, but also as sharing in some special way in the Great High Priesthood of Christ himself.*

Thanks to the Anglican-Roman Catholic International Commission and to such careful inquirers as Professor Wright and Professor Raymond Brown,[19] we have some idea as to what an ordained priest is in the Catholic tradition: a holy person, certainly functionally distinct from the priesthood of the Church, called to be servant, sent forth as apostle, commissioned to manage the affairs of the household of faith (if bishop, to oversee), and authorized to preside at the Holy Eucharist; furthermore, seen historically—from the late second century—to share in some way in, or reflect, Christ's priesthood, specifically in the Eucharistic sacrifice.

The distinction between priests and laypeople was unknown to the New Testament. In fact the concept of an ordained Christian priest was unknown to the New Testament. I do not believe, however, that ordination in itself, or priesthood in itself, stands as contradictory to the New Testament. What *does* stand as contradictory to the New Testament is the priestly *caste* that evolved, in no small part undoubtedly because Church Fathers were inclined to link *function* with *ontology*—specifically, to link the *presbyteroi* with the priesthood and sacrifice of Christ.

I suggest that the ordained ministry of the Catholic Church is *a functional* ministry, and that the ordained priest is set apart from laypeople in a functional way, much in the same way that a doctor, or a janitor, or a rabbi is set apart from people who have not been "called" to his or her particular profession. *In speaking of function in this way, I speak also of sacrament.* What may appear as contradiction is simply paradox. *Ordination is, for me, a sacramental matter.* The call, the education, the examination, the vows, the laying on of hands, the participation of community, the charge, together comprise a profoundly sacramental reality—outward and visible sign of inward and spiritual grace. It is by God's extraordinary grace that something happens in an ordination: the reality of a person's professional presence within the community as priest is "signed, sealed, delivered," as it were—a functional matter; a holy matter. From that day on both the new priest (or deacon, or bishop) and her community of faith are, in some mysterious ways, changed.

I reject the concept of the priest's unique and singular participation in Christ's Great High Priesthood—whether it be representative, iconographic, or a matter of identification. The identification of the priest with Christ is a doctrine perpetuated in order to maintain Priesthood as a *caste*: arrogant and closed, both to new kinds of members and to new theology. Any church doctrine built, maintained and employed to facilitate exclusion and separation rather than inclusion and unity is a doctrine unworthy of the name Jesus Christ. *Perhaps a time will come when women and men, clergy and laity, can agree that, sacramentally speaking, all people are symbolic, representative, even iconographic, of Christ in his priestly sacrifice and otherwise* (much as the New Testament, especially the Fourth Gospel, suggests). To such a doctrine I would say Amen.

NOTES

1. This faith statement is adapted from an address given at Colloquium on "Women and the Priesthood," General Theological Seminary, New York City, February 24, 1975.

2. See Juan Luis Segundo, S.J., *The Sacraments Today* (New York: Maryknoll, 1974).

3. Charles Williams, *Descent into Hell* (New York: Pelligrini and Cuhady, 1949). This novel has since been published in paperback by Eerdmans of Grand Rapids, Michigan.

4. For some eighty-five years prior to 1970, women had been set apart as "deaconesses," considered a separate order from men deacons. Deaconesses had been educated in separate schools from male seminarians and then "set apart" to work in mission fields, Christian education, chaplaincies, or schools. Deaconesses were required to remain single. They were not considered eligible for ordination to the priesthood, although many of the deaconesses believed themselves called by God to the priesthood. Bishop James Pike of California was in 1965 the first bishop to actually permit the *ordination* of a woman deacon, The Rev. Phyllis Edwards, and to declare her a deacon in the same order as men deacons. Five years later, in 1970, the General Convention authorized the ordination of women deacons by declaring that henceforth, deaconesses would be considered deacons on the same basis as men.

5. The statements that follow, about priesthood, were presented, in slightly altered form, as part of an address given at Colloquium on "Women and the Priesthood," General Theological Seminary, New York City, February 24, 1975.

6. See Dorothee Sölle's fine exposition on *phantasie* and obedience in *Beyond Mere Obedience* (Minneapolis: Augsburg, 1970).

7. There are a number of deacons who are, officially, "perpetual deacons." These men and women consider the diaconate to be their vocation. These deacons, and their bishops, understand all along that they do not intend to be priests. They are educated accordingly. The examinations and requirements for the perpetual diaconate are considerably different from, and not as stringent, as the requirements for deacons who plan to be priests. As indicated in footnote 4, there are also a number of deaconesses, women who were "set apart" prior to 1970, when the General Convention first officially opened the diaconate to women on the same basis as men. The deaconesses automatically became deacons in 1970, although a number of them have preferred to retain their identity as "deaconess"—as distinct from deacon. There are other deaconesses, now deacons, who have long believed themselves called to the priesthood.

8. *Services for Trial Use*: Authorized Alternatives to Prayer Book Services (New York: The Church Hymnal Corporation, A Contributing Affiliate of the

Church Pension Fund, 1971), p. 451. This ordinal was used when I was ordained a deacon in 1973.

9. See Article VIII of the Constitution and Canons for the Government of the Protestant Episcopal Church in the United States of America Otherwise Known as The Episcopal Church (adopted in General Conventions), 1789–1973.

10. See Emily C. Hewitt and Suzanne R. Hiatt, *Women Priests: Yes or No?* (New York: Seabury, 1973), for an instructive presentation of the arguments surrounding the issue of women's ordination. Written two years prior to their ordinations as priests.

11. This exercise in imagination is adapted from my article, "A Perspective on Women Priests," in *Leaven*, no. 8 (1974).

12. From a song, "sister: priest (Carter's Song)," written by a student and friend, Jill E. Thompson, New York, 1975; used with permission.

13. The June 22 excerpt from the journal was published in *Christianity and Crisis* 34, no. 15, (September 16, 1974), p. 192.

14. As of this writing, there has been no disciplinary action taken against any of the bishops who ordained us. A mild suspension (three months) was given to one of the eleven women, Katrina Swanson, for her participation in the ordination. None of the others of us have received any official punishment at all. The only Episcopalians who have been taken to church court are Bill Wendt of Washington and Peter Beebe, two of the male priests who have allowed us to celebrate Communion in their parishes. In civil terms, the "accomplices" are being prosecuted and disciplined while the "criminals"–such as we are—sit in the courtrooms, observe the proceedings, and go free.

At this writing, plans for another ordination are underway. On September 7, 1975, God willing, several more women deacons will be ordained to the priesthood.

15. Adaptation of sermon preached at St. Alban's Episcopal Church, Reading, Pa., on Palm Sunday, March 23, 1975; at Christ Episcopal Church, Oberlin, Ohio, on Easter Day, March 30, 1975; and published, in part, as "To Pilate's Great Astonishment," *The Witness* 58, no. 11 (April 27, 1975), p. 2.

16. The Appendix is adapted from my address given at Colloquium on "Women and the Priesthood," General Theological Seminary, New York City, February 24, 1975.

17. The "Canterbury Statement," a paper on "ministry," was produced in 1973 by the Anglican-Roman Catholic International Commission. Its significance will lie in its ecumenical effects. The Canterbury Statement makes no mention of women.

18. J. Robert Wright, "The Canterbury Statement: Background and New Dynamics," Address given April 1, 1974, at Graymoor Conference on Anglican-Roman Catholic Relations.

19. Raymond Brown, S.S., explicates biblical foundations for functions of ordained priesthood and episcopate in *Priest and Bishop: Biblical Reflections* (New York: Paulist Press, 1970).